THE REAL BOOK ABOUT *Indians*

THE *REAL BOOK*

EDITED BY HELEN HOKE

ABOUT *Indians*

BY MICHAEL GORHAM

Illustrated by Fred Collins

GARDEN CITY BOOKS

Garden City, New York

BY ARRANGEMENT WITH FRANKLIN WATTS, INC.

1953

GARDEN CITY BOOKS

Printed in the United States of America

Foreword

WHEN I was a boy in Colorado a good long time ago, the Indian world of the last frontier seemed very close to me. From the mesa on which I lived I could look down on the creek bottom where Arapahoes and the first white settlers had camped peacefully side by side—the whites in their clumsy square tents, and the Arapahoes in their graceful tepees. High above my mesa, near the Continental Divide, I found whole caches of arrowheads along the last line of scrawny trees at timber line.

My Boy Scout master, Ralph Hubbard, had lived among the Plains Indians, and knew their skills and ways of thinking as if he were one of them. He put some of his knowledge down in writing. I knew his book called *Queer Person*. He taught me Indian dances, and I often performed them in delicately worked moccasins, with a gorgeous feather-and-horsehair bustle and flowing eagle-feather bonnet that I wished I had won by real exploits on the Great Plains to the east or in the high game-filled mountain parks to the west.

As I grew older and my travels grew wider, I found a whole undiscovered village where Indians from the pueblos in the Southwest had come to express their awe of the strange and tremendous sand dunes of the San Luis Valley in Colorado. There in the sand lay the corn-grinding stones of a people I had not seen; but see them I must. And I did. Later I saw their ancestral homes in Mesa Verde.

I went out farther over our vast country and traced back to where my grandparents, traveling in a covered wagon, had lived among the first Americans. The road led back farther to the place where *their* grandparents had lived among Indians in New York State—where one had actually lived as a Seneca for many years.

By now my need for knowing about Indians was deep, and I used books, hundreds of them, to bring myself as close to the Indians of the past as I could possibly get. Now as I write my own book about Indians I want to express a debt to every one of them. But a long list of books is for a volume of another kind.

The best I can do here is to express gratitude that a great many scholars have helped me feel that I was in the company of Indians I could not know myself. I have greedily used the information they turned up in their careful studies.

Special thanks for helping me to avoid errors, however, must go to Dr. Ruth Bunzel, anthropologist of Columbia University, who advised me on my manuscript; to Mr. Jack Durham, Mrs. Nita Bradley and Mr. Earl C. Intolubbe of the United States Bureau of Indian Affairs, who read those parts of the manuscript that refer to the Bureau or about which the Bureau has special knowledge; to Mr. Raymond Carlson, editor of *Arizona Highways,* who allowed me to paraphrase parts of an article on Navahos in his publication written by Mr. Cecil Calvin Richardson; to Mrs. Elizabeth Roe-Cloud, Field Secretary of the National Congress of American Indians, who gave valuable information on the problems of Indian life today; and to Oliver La Farge for his expert and sensitive suggestions.

No one of these individuals is responsible for any interpretation of the facts to which they led me. But as you read this book, remember that it has taken a great many people to find out what I have tried to tell—and there is a thousand times more to tell than anyone can set down in one story of the past and present of Indians.

I hope you will go on looking for more of this story. Indians have done a great deal more than most of us realize to make America—North, Central and South—what it is today. And Indians are still very much Americans and they will keep on changing and improving their world, and the world of all of us, just as they have been doing for thousands of years.

MICHAEL GORHAM

Contents

Hopi Indians performed the Snake Dance to bring rain

CHAPTER 1

Redskins and Palefaces

COPPER-SKINNED men, women, and children ran down to the beach on their little tropical island one warm October day long ago. They pointed excitedly at strange-shaped canoes coming toward them. They looked with amazement at three other enormous canoes—surely the biggest anyone had ever seen—that floated farther out in the sea. Each one had big white wings!

But strangest of all were the manlike creatures with pale skins and dark beards who came over the water. They wore heavy, shiny clothes that rattled as they jumped clumsily to the beach. Didn't they know that it was too warm for any clothes at all?

Instead of offering some sign of friendship, like a gift or a pipe to smoke all around, as was customary, these strange creatures drove a stick into the sand. A piece of colored cloth fluttered from its top. This was surely a magic charm of some sort. But these visitors didn't dance around the charm or sing, as people were supposed to do at ceremonies. They just wept and dropped to their knees. And while they knelt they kept holding tight to their spears and enormous shiny knives.

The visitors seemed both very glad and very frightened about something. And when they stood up again, they shouted back and forth to each other with sounds that no one could understand.

No matter how odd the strangers seemed, the copper-skinned islanders knew how to greet anyone who came to their shores. They brought out presents of food and showed by gestures that the newcomers were welcome.

The naked people standing on the beach were looking at the first white men they had ever seen—at the first armor and swords and guns and sailing ships, at the first flag ever carried to their land by a conquering invader. Naturally, they could not look into the future and see that these white men also brought terrible new diseases, and wars that would last four hundred years. So the islanders, who were Arawaks, simply acted polite and friendly. And among themselves they asked: "Who are these creatures on the beach? Are they men, or gods, or devils?"

They weren't gods, of course, or devils either, for that matter—although they soon behaved as if they were. They were simply human beings—men who had dared to sail out into frightening unknown seas. But they were ambitious and greedy men, too. They had come on a long, dangerous voyage looking for wealth, and they were determined to get it, no matter whom they hurt. They were Christopher Columbus and his crew landing on San Salvador, or Watling Island, in 1492.

Columbus gave the name of *Indios* to the copper-skinned Arawaks, because he thought he had reached the land of India for which he had set out. Of course Columbus made an enormous mistake in his geography, but we still use the name he gave to the first tribe of original Americans that he met.

Sometimes people call Indians "redskins," too. This name comes from another mistake. Red was a favorite color the Indians used when they painted their bodies for ceremonies, or for protection against the sun, or to bring good luck in war. Probably the early Spanish sailors told tall tales of the strange new race they had seen in America, and they spoke of red-skinned people when they should have called them copper-colored, or brown.

Back in Spain, Columbus talked about the new world he had discovered, but it wasn't really new. It was very old, and he wasn't the first to discover it. The ancestors of the men and women he met on the beach had done that thousands of years before.

But Columbus did discover a world that was very strange to him and to all who followed after him. It was very different from the one we know today. But it was a world from which palefaces have learned many fascinating and important things.

In this book you will see what Indians were really like in the past and what they are like now. You will go with them as they hunt and dance to please their rain gods, and build great temples covered with gold. You will watch some of their wonderful inventions at work, and you will meet some of the famous Indians doing the things that made them famous.

Finally you will see Indians today building a new life for themselves in this beautiful country that they have always loved and which will always be their home.

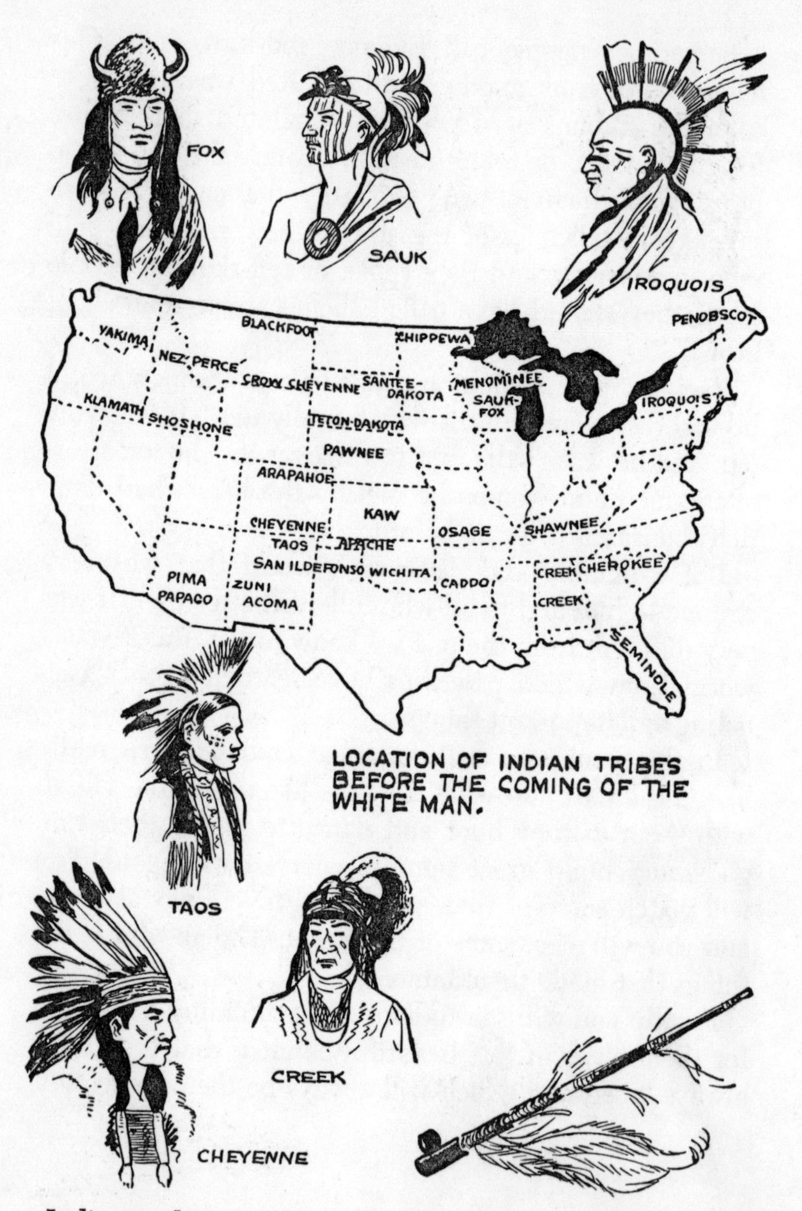

Indians today sometimes put aside their work clothes and wear

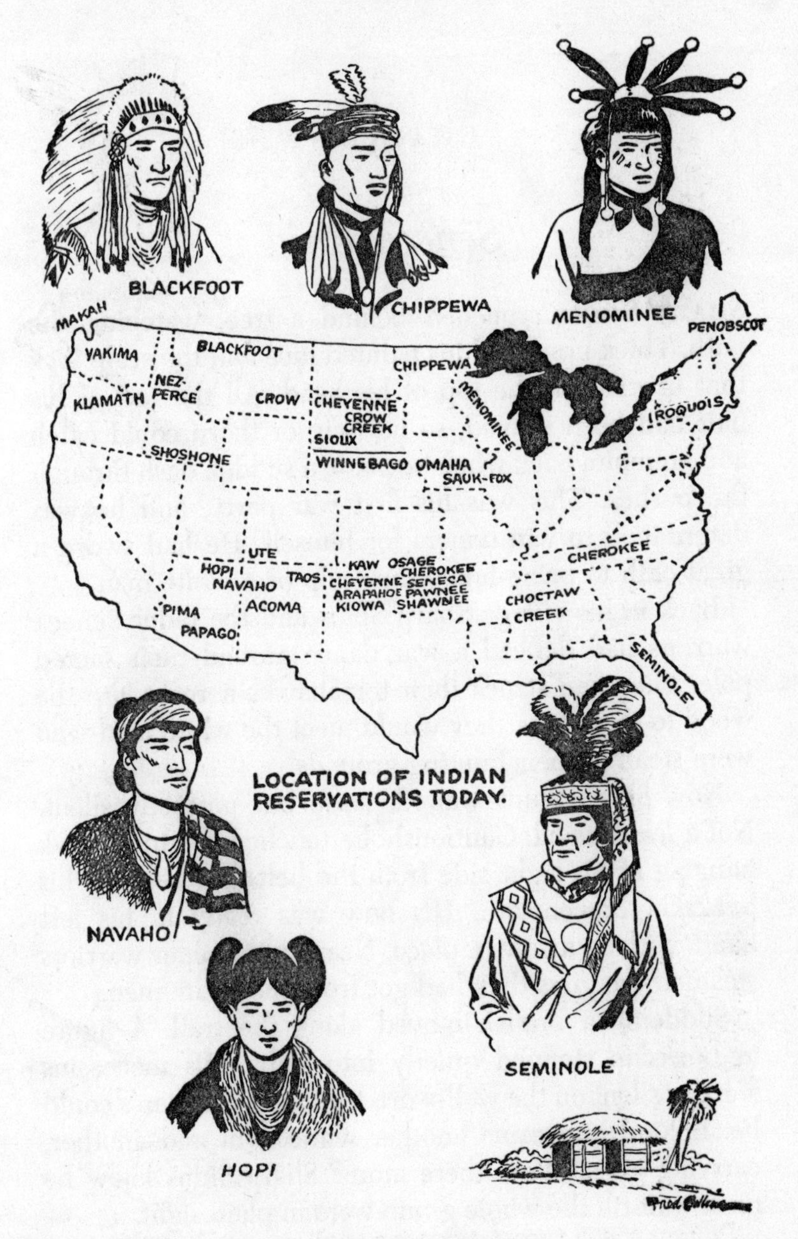

their traditional dress for special ceremonies

CHAPTER 2

Seneca Raid

SHARP SHINS crouched behind a tree, watching the path. Thick brush hid his painted face and the scalp lock that bristled on the top of his head. All the rest of his hair had been shaved, so no twig or thorn could catch and hold him back when he made a sudden dash through the bushes. This was his first war party, and he was determined to win honors for himself. He had sworn a great oath to bring home the scalp of a white man.

Back in his village Sharp Shins and the older Seneca warriors had danced a war dance around their sacred pole. They had struck their tomahawks fiercely into the wood to show how they would meet the white men who were stealing their hunting grounds.

Now Sharp Shins waited, tense but perfectly silent. Not a leaf moved. Cautiously he touched the tomahawk hanging at his right side from the belt that held up his buckskin breechcloth. His bow was ready in his left hand, with an arrow in place. Near by the older warriors steadied the guns they had got from the white men.

Suddenly a branch moved along the trail. A figure in buckskin stepped quietly into sight. His moccasins were as silent on the well-worn trail as any Indian's could be. Behind him came another white man and another, carrying guns. Were there more? Sharp Shins knew he must wait till the whole group were in plain sight.

At last the Seneca chief gave a signal with his hand. Sharp Shins shot his arrow. At the same instant, the other warriors fired guns or arrows and gave their piercing war cries.

Sharp Shins' arrow found its target, and in a flash he had his victim's scalp. Bursting with pride and courage, he swung his tomahawk at another man who had raised his gun to shoot. The tomahawk missed but knocked the gun to the ground. The white man was no coward. He turned toward Sharp Shins, reaching for his own tomahawk. But Sharp Shins was too quick. He knocked the tomahawk away and tried for a wrestler's hold.

The white man twisted away from him, turned, and fled off the trail into the woods. Sharp Shins followed. But although Sharp Shins had won his name because he was such a good runner, the white man escaped. Full of shame and anger, Sharp Shins returned to his war party. The battle was over. Warriors were taking the best knives and guns from the fallen enemy and tying the hands of four captives.

SEARCH

"There is another in the woods," Sharp Shins told the chief. "We must get him so he cannot spread an alarm."

A small group of warriors set off with Sharp Shins to track the one man who had escaped the ambush. They sped through the forest, following every sign—a broken twig, grass bent under a moccasin, an overturned pebble. At last they found him, cleverly hidden in some brush.

Now Sharp Shins looked at the captive in surprise. This was no man—only a young fellow about his own age, fifteen or sixteen. Sharp Shins was angrier than ever. He wanted to kill the boy who had outrun him.

But an older warrior, Stubborn One, said: "No. We must keep him as a captive. If he is brave, he will make a good son for my sister Falling Leaf, whose own son was lost in our last raid." Now Stubborn One put a string of sacred shells, called wampum, around the boy's neck and motioned for him to come along, back to the trail.

HANDSOME BOY

All the other warriors looked at the new captive with interest. The wampum around his neck told them he must not be harmed—for the present, at least. They were impressed by his quickness and his good looks. Handsome Boy became the captive's name, and he was to have it for a long time.

The Senecas put everything they had to carry on the backs of Handsome Boy and the other prisoners. Then they started north as fast as they could travel. By day they followed the trail along the tops of ridges where they could keep a lookout for enemies. At night they camped and slept, after tying the prisoners' feet to logs so they could not escape. Handsome Boy seemed to keep up his strength and courage, although his pack was heavy and his hands were bound.

Sharp Shins wondered a little about this white boy who strode along without showing any signs of unfriendliness. In fact, he wondered about all white men and their peculiar ways. The first ones he had known were dressed in buckskins, like Handsome Boy. They had invaded his tribe's hunting grounds in western Pennsylvania. In the beginning, they had made a treaty about the use of the land, but time and again they broke it.

PROMISES

Later, some other white men had come to Sharp Shins' tribe from the north. Their leader said they were soldiers for the English king. These King's men were at war with the buckskin-clad Pennsylvanians. If the Senecas would join in the war, the King's men said they would give them back the Indian lands that the Pennsylvanians had stolen.

The Seneca chiefs had listened in silence. Who could believe the promises of any white man? But the leader of the King's men produced a good argument. He had soldiers right here, ready to fight. If his men were willing to die in battle alongside the Indians, wasn't that proof enough that they would keep their word?

The Seneca warriors were convinced. They agreed to help. They would send war parties against the Pennsylvanians. Now Sharp Shins and his companions were bringing back prisoners. They would get a reward for each captive and each scalp they turned over to the King's men. It seemed to them that they had made a good bargain. They were defending their lands and getting paid for doing so.

At last the trail led into a clearing among the trees, and there stood a tall fence of upright logs, surrounding the Indian village called Painted Post. Inside the log palisade, the warriors felt safe. They were among friends, so they stopped and held a victory dance around the painted post that gave the village its name. For the first time Sharp Shins could boast of his feat in battle, showing the scalp he had taken from the hated white invaders.

ADVANCE WARNING

Next day the war party pushed on farther north toward Sharp Shins' own village. As they approached it, Stubborn One began to talk with Handsome Boy in broken English. Soon, he said, Handsome Boy would have to show his courage if he wanted to live. Up to now, no harm had come to him because he wore the wampum string. The wampum belonged to the warrior's sister Falling Leaf, who was waiting at the village in the hope that there would be a captive brave enough for her to adopt as her own son. To prove himself, Handsome Boy would have to run the gauntlet. The wampum belt had protected him so far, but when he ran the gauntlet he would be on his own.

Sharp Shins saw that Handsome Boy showed no fear—even when Stubborn One explained the gauntlet. The boy would have to run between two lines of men and women and children who would all try to strike him with clubs or whips—perhaps even with tomahawks. The Senecas wanted no weaklings to adopt in place of their own fallen warriors. They might try to kill any man who showed fear or was struck down. But they would take every care of one who could run the gauntlet bravely and without being hurt. He would be safe if he ran into the Long House at the end of the test.

The war party went on through the forest in silence again. Then suddenly they all gave a great shout, calling out news of their victory to the village. People streamed from the large, barnlike, bark-covered houses, grabbing anything for weapons as they came. In no time they had lined up in two rows that stretched from the river below the town up to the entrance of the Long House, which stood in the center of the village.

Sharp Shins dashed off to get a place in line. He still felt angry that he had been outrun and had needed help in capturing an enemy no older than he was. Now he would have another chance at Handsome Boy.

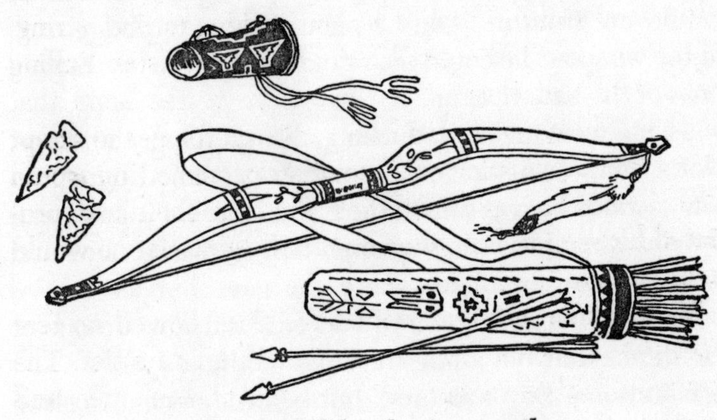

Weapons used by the forest tribes

CHAPTER 3

Sharp Shins and His White Brother

HANDSOME BOY looked carefully at the ground he had to run over. He noted every clump of grass so that he would not stumble. And he planned how to dodge each of the weapons he could see brandished in the two ragged lines of the gauntlet run.

Then, weaving and ducking, he sped up the slope. Not a whip or a stick or a tomahawk touched him! In a few seconds he was safe in the Long House. Falling Leaf, the old woman whose wampum belt he wore, came and took him to her lodge. There she gave him corn-meal mush with maple sugar and laid out bearskins on one of the bunks that ran along the sides of the lodge.

Handsome Boy was tired, but before he went to sleep he looked curiously at his new home. Above his lower bunk was another, obviously used for storage and not for sleeping. Around the room were many other bunks. Several families must share this place with Falling Leaf.

Outside, Sharp Shins walked around telling people of his first triumph in battle, and waiting for the victory dance to begin. Later he joined in the dance, all decked out with turtle-shell rattles tied to his knees, designs painted on his body, and the scalp he had taken tied to his belt. As he danced he acted out his part in the fight, offering thanks to the spirits for his victory.

SACHEMS IN THE LONG HOUSE

Once he looked up and saw Falling Leaf coming from the Long House. Sharp Shins knew what this meant. The sachems—leaders who were in charge of peaceful things—would soon start discussing the adoption of Handsome Boy. After dancing some more, Sharp Shins stepped inside the Long House to watch the sachems make their decision. Stubborn One, who had helped capture Handsome Boy, told the story of the battle all over again, told how brave Handsome Boy had been, how Falling Leaf needed a son to replace the son whom the white men had killed. He said Handsome Boy was a bold fighter, and could surely learn to be a good hunter who would keep plenty of meat in the old woman's lodge. It seemed that the Great Spirit had sent Handsome Boy on purpose to take the place of Falling Leaf's son. Many sachems talked after this, and all agreed to the adoption. Handsome Boy should become a Seneca, even though they would lose the King's reward for him.

Everyone joined in singing an old Seneca song, and the sachems gave the captive his official name. It was the one he had already received at the time of his capture—Handsome Boy. Now the Senecas considered him a full-blooded member of the tribe.

MANY BROTHERS AND SISTERS

Every Seneca belonged not only to the tribe as a whole but also to a clan within the tribe. Handsome Boy's new mother belonged to the Hawk Clan, and so he did, too. The other boys and girls in the clan were all his brothers and sisters or cousins. Among them was Sharp Shins.

Even Sharp Shins joined in welcoming Handsome Boy. He put aside the hatred he had felt after the battle and began to show Handsome Boy some of the things he would need to know in his strange adopted home.

Together the new brothers wandered about the town, and Sharp Shins explained how everything was done. The women, with babies on their backs in cradle boards, worked in the cornfields and sang together as they weeded and dug the soil. They pounded the dried kernels into meal, using a hollowed-out tree stump to hold the corn. They boiled squash and beans and corn in pots made of bark that hung over the heat of the fire but not too near the flame.

As they looked around, Sharp Shins taught his brother the Seneca words for everything. Before long Handsome Boy could ask for maple syrup, and he knew how it was made of sap drained from maple trees into bark buckets, then boiled till it became sugar. He saw hunters go off with bearskin pouches full of the rich sugar mixed with parched corn. It was all the food they needed for a long trip.

Sharp Shins learned things, too. Handsome Boy taught him how to repair a gun and how to pound pieces of silver English money into decorations. Together they went hunting for deer. Sharp Shins knew just where to find the trails that deer used when they went for water or for salt to lick. It wasn't long before old Falling Leaf had plenty of deerskins to make into clothes.

The two boys liked to watch her prepare the skins. She used a stone scraper to take off the hair. Then she

A Seneca village

smeared the skin with the deer's brains to make it soft. Later, when it was clean and dry and as soft as velvet, Falling Leaf cut it up into leggings for Handsome Boy to wear in winter. The leggings were like pants without any seat, and she sewed them with deer sinew and covered the cuffs and seams with decorations made of colored glass beads she had got from English traders.

Falling Leaf made a buckskin hunting jacket too, and decorated it. She made moccasins decorated with tiny bone buttons and beads and gay-colored porcupine quills. Before long Handsome Boy was dressed like a Seneca. He and Sharp Shins had long talks in the Seneca language.

Sharp Shins explained customs that seemed very strange to Handsome Boy. Fathers weren't very important inside a Seneca house, but mothers were. They owned the house and all the things in it. No husband ever tried to tell his wife how to run her home. She was boss there. Women sometimes even got together and chose new sachems for their clans, and a woman was head of one of the men's secret groups—the False Face Club.

FALSE FACE CLUB

To understand this strange club, Handsome Boy had to learn first what the Senecas thought was the cause of sickness. They believed that queer, ugly, bodiless faces flew about spreading diseases and all kinds of evil. So a group of people in each village were organized to fight these disease spirits. They masked themselves in false faces even more hideous than the faces of the spirits.

Now when a sick person dreamed about one of the evil flying heads, he told the mistress of the False Face Club and asked the women to prepare a feast. Then, wearing their masks, the False Faces marched into the patient's lodge. They stirred the ashes of the fire, sprinkled them over the head of the patient, and performed a special dance. The patient joined in. When the dance was finished, each False Face carried away his share of the feast and ate it alone. Only the mistress of the club knew the members. They never unmasked in public, or even among themselves.

Spring and fall were the times for the great False Face ceremonies, for these were the seasons of sickness. From house to house the False Faces went, carrying rattles made of snapping-turtle shells. They made all kinds of weird sounds, to frighten off any evil spirits that might be lurking about the village.

There was no doubt that Seneca women had a very important place in the tribe. Sharp Shins hardly believed Handsome Boy's report that white women were not supposed to be the equals of men. Handsome Boy agreed that men should do the hunting and fighting. But he wasn't at all sure yet that they should allow women to have so many privileges.

SNOW SNAKE

It had been summertime when Sharp Shins first pursued Handsome Boy through the woods. Now in the fall they chased each other at games and competed in races. The fleetest boys and young men served as messengers who carried news from one village to another. A good runner could cover as much as a hundred miles in a day.

When winter came, they played Snow Snake. Dressed in jacket and leggings and warm skin robes, the men and boys skidded slender poles over the hard-crusted snow. The one who sent his snow-snake pole the farthest was the winner. Sharp Shins was so skillful that he could make his snow snake go a quarter of a mile.

Winter was the season when everyone had most time to spare, particularly if the fall hunting had been good. So, late in January, the Senecas held a big midwinter festival that lasted a week. The boys could hardly wait for it to begin, because though they always got into mischief at the festival, nobody ever scolded them. Dressed as warriors, the older ones went from house to house, dancing a war dance and giving their war whoops. Behind them ran younger boys wearing masks. An old woman tagged along, carrying a huge basket.

At every lodge, the boys begged for presents to put in the basket. If they liked the presents, they did a dance and went away. But if anybody was stingy, trouble started. The boys grabbed whatever they could put their hands on and ran. Next day they laid out all the things they had taken. Any old grouch who had the courage to admit that an article was his could get it back by paying a ransom of food.

Then in the early spring there came a great time of games and feasting—the Maple Festival when people began to gather maple-tree sap and offered thanks to the trees for giving the sweet juice.

MAPLE-SYRUP TIME

Sachems chose the time for the festival, and people from many villages gathered for work in the woods. They slashed the tree trunks so that the sap would run down to a sort of spout at the bottom and then into a bark tub.

Bark pots full of sap steamed over fires at the edge

of the woods, and toward evening the syrup began to thicken. Then the women poured it into cooling molds. Some of the molds had designs cut into them, just the way maple-sugar candy molds have to this day.

Often there were still banks of snow in the shady woods. The women ladled some of the hot syrup onto the snow, where it quickly hardened. The children kept running up and begging for the treat.

In the evening, everybody enjoyed a feast of cornmeal cakes and hot syrup. Then they sat up late, talking, arguing, and joking.

LACROSSE

Along with the feasting and the fun came ceremonies and games. The most important game was something like lacrosse. Sharp Shins and Handsome Boy had been training to play it for a long time. Each one had a stick with a net attached to a curve at the end of it. He used the net to catch a ball and then toss it back. Hour after hour the two boys played catch and practised running and trying to knock the ball out of each other's nets.

At the festival, dozens of players from two villages lined up. Men and boys, and sometimes women too, stood opposite each other on the mile-long field. Sharp Shins had painted a streak of lightning on his chest, and on Handsome Boy he had drawn a running deer. He said the pictures would help them win.

The boys took their places at the back of the field, where the fastest runners were needed. The strongest men stood at the center of the field, where there would be the roughest fighting. The game *was* rough. Players struggled to get the ball. They could wrestle, trip opponents, bang them over the head with the sticks. But no one could complain about getting hurt. If a player was knocked down, he jumped up laughing, even if he had a bloody nose. Any sign of anger brought a yell of "Coward!" from the crowd of people watching. A player felt very much ashamed if he was hurt so badly that he had to leave the game.

This was a sport for men who must be able to bear great hardships while they were hunting or in battle. Handsome Boy became one of the best of the players. Hardship was no new thing to him. Life in the white village where he had grown up was just about as rough and ready as anything he found among the Senecas. Although he was homesick at times, he came to like his new family and friends very much. The people here were as generous and honest with each other as he thought any people could ever be. And so, like other captured white boys and girls, he stayed on happily with the Senecas for many, many years.

(The story of Sharp Shins can be found in a few old books, but that's not where the author heard it first. He heard it from his grandmother, and she was the great-granddaughter of Handsome Boy. Most of the customs that Handsome Boy adopted when he became a Seneca were very useful in the forest, and they were similar to the customs of all the groups we now call Eastern Woodland Indians.)

CHAPTER 4

Sitting Bull

"SLOW" was the boy's nickname—in fact, the only name he'd ever had in all his fourteen years. But there was nothing slow about the way he rode away from the circle of tepees in his village. When he was sure no grownups could see him, he whipped up his fast pony and headed straight for the place where he knew he would find his father. Slow had overheard the plans that his father and the other warriors in the Hunkpapa band of Sioux were making for a raid on their rivals, the Crows. Now he was determined to join the men as they went off to win honors—and horses—from the Crows.

Of course nobody had asked him to go along. Slow was still a boy. Nobody expected him to do much of anything but play games and run races and wrestle, and study nature while he was hunting birds and small animals. People called him Slow because he always took his time to think things over. But once he had made up his mind, he was quick enough. Now he had decided to be the first boy of his age to go out with a raiding party.

Hadn't he killed his first buffalo when he was ten? That was long before any of his playmates had dared ride up to one of the big beasts and send an arrow into its ribs. Perhaps a battle took more daring than a buffalo hunt. But Slow knew that war was as much a game as it was a way of stealing horses or keeping other tribes away from your hunting grounds. The point in a battle was to win honors rather than to kill enemies. Courage was more important than killing, and Slow was going to show that he had courage enough to be considered a man.

His father was surprised to see Slow. But he was pleased, very pleased, when he found out what the boy wanted. He urged Slow to do something brave and he handed him his own coup stick.

That coup stick was Slow's only weapon. Actually, it wasn't a weapon at all. It was just a harmless piece of wood, decorated with duck feathers, which a warrior held in his hand. The whole idea was to dash up and touch a living enemy with the stick. This took much more courage than simply staying at a distance and shooting arrows. And so it was the greatest possible honor to touch an enemy—a much greater honor than to kill him.

Before long, scouts brought word that a band of Crows was coming straight toward Slow's party. "Prepare for battle," they warned. The men took covers from buffalo-hide shields and got bows, lances, and coup sticks ready.

THE FIRST COUP

Slow paid no attention to the men. He stood by himself, covering his entire body with yellow paint. Next he smeared red paint all over his gray horse. Then, before anybody realized what he was doing, he leaped into the little buffalo-skin saddle that was stuffed with dried grass. His moccasined feet found the stirrups, and he was off in the direction of the approaching Crows. The men followed when they saw him start, but the boy's fast pony kept ahead of them.

The surprised Crows turned and fled—all except one

man, who jumped from his horse and stood waiting for Slow with bow and arrow in his hand ready to shoot.

Slow didn't hesitate. He urged his horse faster, straight toward the fearless Crow. Just in time the boy swung his coup stick, hit the enemy's bow, and spoiled his aim. Then Slow did what he knew every grown man was supposed to do when he had touched a living enemy.

"I, Slow," he shouted, "have conquered him!"

Slow had counted his first coup. And he had won greater honors than any of the grown men, because he had been in the very forefront of the attack.

A MAN'S NAME

Now the time had come, everyone agreed, to treat Slow as a man. That meant he should have a real man's name. Names were sacred things to the Sioux, and Slow's father had in mind one that was especially sacred. It had come in a vision once when he was out hunting with three other men. He said that a bull buffalo wandered up close to the hunters and then spoke four names. Buffalo were the most important things in the lives of the Sioux, because the animals gave them most of their food, clothes, tools, and shelter. They believed there was a buffalo god. So if a buffalo spoke, his words were important.

Two of the sacred words that the buffalo uttered in the vision were "Sitting Bull." Slow's father took them for his own name, and he valued them highly. He had nothing more precious to offer his son—so he gave Slow this sacred name of his. That is how the boy everyone called Slow got his man's name, Sitting Bull.

From now on, scarcely a year went by when he was not in the forefront of some battle. Often he made several coups in one year. Always the man who bore the sacred name given by the buffalo showed the qualities of the buffalo. He was fearless and strong. He kept straight on doing what he had decided to do.

All the honors Sitting Bull won made him very important among the Hunkpapa Sioux. Everybody respected him, but more than that, everybody liked him.

People liked Sitting Bull because of his quiet, friendly ways. He was a good hunter, and he always had meat to give families who didn't have any. He was always smiling and laughing, and he never showed off with fine clothes. He could have strutted around wearing a lot of feathers for all the coups he had made, but he didn't. Any old moccasins and buckskin breechcloth were good enough for him. Sitting Bull knew he was a good warrior and hunter, but he didn't put on airs.

CHIEF OF THE STRONG HEARTS

Before long Sitting Bull was elected a member of the Strong Hearts, a special society of the best warriors. Then he was chosen to be one of the two members called sash-wearers. This gave him the right to put on a headdress covered with crow feathers cut short and decorated with buffalo horns. His red sash, also decorated with feathers, was so long that it dragged on the ground.

When a sash-wearer got into battle, he jumped off his horse and staked himself to the ground by driving his lance through the long red sash. There he had to fight, for he was too proud to pull the lance out and run from danger. Then a sash-wearer could move only when one of his friends came and yanked the lance away.

To be made a sash-wearer was a very high honor indeed. But there was one still higher, and Sitting Bull won that, too. He became leader of the Midnight Strong Hearts—the best of all warriors in the Strong Hearts.

As leader, Sitting Bull had a most important job to do. He was in charge of all the hunting arrangements for the Hunkpapa Sioux. The Hunkpapas never went hungry, although the hunters had to kill three thousand buffalo a year to keep their families fed.

THE WARRIOR SIOUX

The Hunkpapa band was only one of many Sioux bands. It was part of the Teton division of the great Sioux or Dakota nation whose people wandered all over the northern plains. Two-Kettle, Minniconjou, Oglalla, and Sans Arc were the names of some of the other Teton Sioux bands. All of them were friendly with one another, but they hunted separately, each with its own chief.

Until the white men began to come, there were buffalo enough for all the Sioux, with plenty besides for neighboring tribes like Crows, Rees, Hidatsas, and others. That's why Indian wars were somewhat like games, rather than being desperate fights to survive.

But now things were changing. The white men killed tens of thousands of buffalo just for the hides. White settlers and soldiers pushed Indians out of their old hunting grounds into Teton Sioux territory in South Dakota. The Sioux had to fight more and more fiercely against their old enemies—and against the whites, too.

At first, each band fought its own separate battles, without any plan. Then they began to see that they would be better off if they all co-operated. But if they were to fight together, they needed one chief over them all. Who would be the best leader? Everywhere in the Teton Sioux camps the fame of one chief had spread. Everyone talked of Sitting Bull and the battle he had won against a big party of Crows all by himself. This is how it happened:

Two Crows had charged in among the Sioux. One of them killed a Sioux warrior and the other counted two coups. Then Sitting Bull rode out to meet a third Crow who was charging. To show his fearlessness, Sitting Bull jumped off his horse and sent it galloping away. Then he challenged the Crow, who was a chief, to single combat.

Both men had old muzzle-loading rifles. As Sitting Bull dropped to his knee to take aim, the Crow fired. His bullet hit Sitting Bull's left foot. But Sitting Bull's aim was better. He killed the Crow chief. The Sioux warriors, shouting praises, charged the other Crows, who fled.

Sitting Bull's wound healed, but it left a bad scar, so that he limped all the rest of his life.

TETON CHIEF

By now some of the Cheyennes and the Arapahoes wanted to co-operate with the Teton Sioux. And so they all got together in a great meeting to elect one chief.

Thousands of Indians gathered. They set up a big council lodge. Then four leading men took a buffalo robe to Sitting Bull's tepee. On it they carried him to the place of honor in the council lodge. There they lit a ceremonial pipe, decorated with duck feathers, and pointed it toward the earth, then toward the four winds, and then to the sky. After that the pipe went around the lodge and each leader puffed at it in turn, saying a prayer to Wakan Tanka, the Great Spirit.

Sitting Bull was now chief of all the Teton bands, and

everyone celebrated with joyous dances and songs. Warriors decked themselves out in war paint. They put on eagle-feather headdresses. Men who had killed bears wore necklaces of bears' claws. And Sitting Bull rode among the people on a great white horse they had given him to show him their love.

YEARS OF PEACE

Sitting Bull had a plan for leading his people. He decided they must protect their hunting grounds from other Indian tribes, but they must never start war with the whites. If the whites shot first, of course he was determined to fight back. He made a treaty with the United States Government that set aside most of western South Dakota as a reservation where no white men except traders were permitted.

The plan worked, and there were years of peace. But the Government broke the treaty and sent soldiers into the reservation. One of them was General George Custer, whom the Indians called Long Hair. Custer traveled deep into the Black Hills, and there one day he found gold.

Now trouble really began. Custer bragged about the gold. White men poured into the Indians' country. Even with so many invaders seizing the land, Sitting Bull tried to prevent war. But when at last an army came and started shooting, he gathered all the tribes together in order to fight back. Quickly his warriors defeated the white army and sent it running away from Sioux territory.

When Custer found out that all the tribes were assembled in one place, he thought he saw a chance to make himself famous—perhaps even become President of the United States. People back East had been told that the Sioux were wicked, dangerous, treacherous enemies who would not live in peace. The fact was, of course, that the Sioux wanted only to be let alone. But when they weren't, they were the most skillful and courageous of all Indian warriors. Nothing would make Custer seem like more of a hero than to defeat Sitting Bull.

So Custer led his army into Sioux territory against Sitting Bull's encampment of five large bands. Custer planned to attack from two sides, but he had not realized what great warriors the Sioux were and how bravely they would fight. His army was defeated, and he, together with all the men he commanded in the last attack died.

Now Sitting Bull saw that there could be no living at peace with the white men in the United States. So he led many of his people into Canada, where the American soldiers could not follow and try to get revenge.

Sitting Bull had no fear for himself when he retreated. Fear was not in him. But he did want to save his people. Always he did the best he could think of for those who had asked him to be their leader. Many of the chiefs under him were richer in ponies than he ever was, because he kept making presents to others who were in need. And every man, whether Indian or white, who really knew him respected his honesty. Sitting Bull kept every agreement he made. When he fought against the soldiers, it was always they who started the fighting. Today many people say that Sitting Bull was the greatest man who ever lived in South Dakota.

Plains Indians prepared to fight the white man's army

CHAPTER 5

Kidnapped

EARLY ONE MORNING all the young men in the small band of Shoshones rode out to hunt. Only the older men and boys stayed with the women and children in the little group of tepees near the creek.

As the hunters left, a pretty teen-age girl picked up the elk-skin blanket she had slept in and pulled it around her shoulders as a robe. With the fringes of her antelope-skin leggings dragging in the damp grass, she walked to the edge of the creek, her sharp digging stick in her hand.

The slender girl's name was Sacajawea, which meant Boat Woman, and her eyes were as sharp as the stick she used in digging up roots to be dried for winter food. As she waited for the other women, she looked at the landmarks all around her and put them away in her memory. It was good that she did. Two of the most important things that ever happened to her were going to happen at this very spot.

Off to the west rose high, snow-covered mountains. Sacajawea had crossed over them, and she knew the swift big river that flowed down on the other side. Here, near her camp, three creeks joined and became the Missouri River—the Muddy Water.

Suddenly Sacajawea looked intently. Something on a rise in the plain had caught her eye, something that moved. In a moment she knew that what she had seen meant danger—a war party of the Hidatsa tribe.

"BIG BELLIES!"

"Big Bellies! Big Bellies!" she called out. (That was another name for Hidatsas or Gros Ventres.)

Everyone rushed from the tepees. The few men in camp ran for the horses that were grazing close by with their bridle ropes ready around their necks. Women snatched up the children. If the Big Bellies attacked, the Shoshones could only try to get away, for all the strong young warriors were hunting. The old men could not fight off a real war party.

But now they hesitated. Nothing seemed to be happening. There was no sign of the enemy. Perhaps Sacajawea had given a false alarm. Just as they decided that she had, there came a terrible yelling. Horses dashed from around both sides of a low hill, and the Big Belly warriors rode straight for the camp. Some of them had guns in their hands.

Sacajawea and the others leaped on their horses and headed toward the forest three miles away. They had a good start, and there was a chance they could hide themselves in the thick woods before it was too late.

Galloping as fast as they could, they spread out over the open land along the creek. But the Hidatsas gained on them. They had no time to hide. The Big Belly warriors killed all the old men and most of the boys.

In the thick of the fight, Sacajawea felt a long lance poking at her. The painted warrior who held it shouted in a strange tongue and motioned for her to turn around and ride back to the creek. She was a captive. So were the other women and girls and most of the horses.

At the creek the Big Bellies drove them across a shallow place. Then they rode all day and all night, as hard as the horses could be pushed. The Big Bellies wanted to get away before the Shoshone warriors on their tough mountain horses could catch up.

Then, moving more slowly, the Hidatsas and their captives followed the Missouri River downstream for days and days. Sacajawea had to ride bareback. She had had no time to get her little buffalo-skin saddle when the Big Bellies raided her camp. Now she was very stiff, and so tired she could scarcely stay on her horse, and the horse could scarcely put one foot in front of the other. She was even glad to see the Hidatsa village at last, with its strange round, mud-covered log huts. Although this was the enemy's village, it would be a place to rest.

When the captured women and horses came in, the whole village began to celebrate, but Sacajawea paid little attention. Before long some women took her into a hut, which was partly underground and much larger than the skin-covered tepees she was used to. There, on the earth floor, was a soft buffalo robe to lie on, and she fell asleep.

STRANGE NEW WAYS

After Sacajawea had rested she left the hut and was given some roasted buffalo meat with boiled squash and baked corncakes. She had never tasted squash and corn before, but she liked them.

Then the Hidatsa women gave her work to do. The words they used when they talked to her were strange, but most of the tasks were like the ones she had always done. She gathered wood and cooked. She scraped skins and sewed them into clothing.

One kind of work, though, was entirely new to Sacajawea. Every day she went with the other women to dig in the fields where corn and squash grew. The Shoshones had always got their food by hunting and fishing and gathering roots and berries. The Hidatsas did all these things, but they also made food grow for them. And this, Sacajawea realized, was a wonderful idea indeed.

As she learned about farming, she learned the Hidatsa language. Everyone treated her well—just as if she had always been a member of the tribe. Sacajawea was beginning to feel at home.

SOLD INTO SLAVERY

Then one day a strange-looking man came to the village. He had white skin and a beard. Sacajawea had never seen a beard before. Indian men didn't have much hair on their faces. The stranger bought furs from the Hidatsas and gave them beads and mirrors, knives and tomahawks, in exchange. And when he saw Sacajawea he wanted to buy her, too. For a long time he bargained with Black Moccasin, the Hidatsa chief. Finally they agreed on a price.

Sacajawea moved on to another village of round, mud-covered log huts and became the slave and wife of the French trader, Toussaint Charbonneau. She was getting farther and farther away from the high mountain country of her own people.

Now she lived with the Mandan tribe, who wore earrings of big brilliant-colored beads that they made by a secret process no white man ever learned, and scarcely a month went by that she didn't meet some new kind of Indian—Arikaras, Assiniboins, Chippewas.

HORSES IN THE HOUSE

Once some Cheyennes came to smoke the pipe of peace with the Mandans. But the Mandans were at war with the Sioux. Often people in Sacajawea's village took their best horses right into the big log huts at night to keep them from being stolen by Sioux raiders.

Sacajawea came to like many things about her new life. Mandans had more food than she had ever seen. Some of their recipes were wonderful, too. She particularly liked a dish of pumpkin, beans, corn, and chokecherries all boiled together.

Then one autumn day—the year was 1804—Charbonneau took her to see some white men who were staying in another Mandan village. She gave them buffalo robes as a sign of friendship and then sat down to listen.

The strangers spoke English to an interpreter who spoke French to her husband. Sacajawea couldn't understand a word they said. She could only speak Shoshone and Hidatsa and a little Mandan, but she could tell that some of the talk was about herself. In the end it was all decided: Sacajawea and her husband were to go as guides and interpreters with an expedition all the way up the Missouri River, across the great mountains, and down the westward-flowing river—the Columbia—that she remembered from long ago. The leader of the expedition, Captain Lewis, particularly wanted Sacajawea to go along, even though she was to have a baby soon.

She could help them make friends with her people, the Shoshones, whom they called the Snake Indians because they often hunted along the Snake River. It was especially important for Lewis and his assistant Captain William Clark to make friends with the Shoshones. The white men needed to get some tough, strong horses from the Indians for their trip across the Rocky Mountains. They wanted Sacajawea along for another reason, too. If Indians they met along the way saw an Indian woman, they would realize that this was not a war party.

BABY IN A BASKET

During the winter, Sacajawea's baby was born, and she wove a kind of basket for him that she carried on her back. The men prepared big boats to take them up the Missouri on the first part of their long journey.

Sacajawea would be the only woman in a party of more than thirty men, and the only Indian for much of the way. All the others were white except a man whose name was York. His skin was much darker than her own. He too had black hair, but it was very curly instead of straight like hers. This dark-skinned man was a Negro slave who had been bought just as she had been.

Sacajawea was curious about York. She had seen the skins of Indians painted so many different colors that she thought he must be painted too. She wet her finger and rubbed it on his skin to see if the black would come off. It didn't. Sacajawea was beginning to learn how many different kinds of people there are in the world.

At last everything was ready. One spring day Sacajawea put her baby into his basket, strapped it on her back, and began one of the most famous of all journeys.

CHAPTER 6

The Captive Returns

SACAJAWEA knew that her job was important. She had to help lead Lewis and Clark through the great Western country that had never been seen by white men before. President Jefferson had sent these men to explore a vast area he had just bought from France—and he wanted to know what lay beyond the new land, too. Also, Jefferson ordered the explorers to make friends with the Indians wherever they went.

The party set out in two large river boats that had sails and oars, and there were six buffalo-skin canoes, too. The boats carried bales and bales of food, clothing, guns, ammunition, and all kinds of beads, cloth, tomahawks, mirrors, and other things to give the Indians.

Thoughts of meeting her own people again filled Sacajawea with excitement. She began to remember many things that she hadn't seen or done in the five years that she had been a captive. One evening, after the boats pulled up to the shore and the men started making camp, she took a sharp pointed stick—just the kind she'd been using the day she was captured. Then she walked along the riverbank looking for piles of driftwood. Near each pile she poked the stick into the ground. When it sank in quickly, she knew she had found an animal burrow. With her stick she opened the burrow up and pulled out handfuls of tender wild artichokes that the animals had stored there.

The white men ate the strange vegetables and liked them. Later she brought them buckets full of delicious wild berries. Sacajawea was going to be helpful in more ways than one. She could get food that the white men would never know how to find by themselves. The Shoshones had learned ways of gathering food in even the most barren parts of their Rocky Mountain home.

RESCUE

One day Sacajawea's boat almost tipped over. Everything spilled out—including the precious records of the trip that Lewis and Clark had been keeping to give to President Jefferson. Sacajawea was sitting toward the back of the boat. Somehow she managed to hold on to the side with one hand while she reached out with the other and caught the records as they floated past. By her calmness she saved the one thing that meant most to the explorers.

Another time it was Sacajawea herself who was almost lost in the river. With her baby on her back, she had left her boat and was walking ahead of it with her husband Charbonneau, Clark, and York. Just where the river cut through steep canyon walls they looked up and saw a great rainstorm coming. York climbed to the top of the cliffs to hunt for shelter. The others stopped under an overhanging rock to stay out of the rain.

But more than rain came. A great flash flood roared down the canyon in a tremendous wall of water. Before they realized what was happening, water swirled around their feet. Soon it would rise and wash them away. Charbonneau turned and ran, leaving his wife and baby. Sacajawea held the baby high in her arms and tried to scramble up the steep canyon. Her foot slipped and she almost lost her balance. In another moment she would have been trapped by the raging flood. But behind her stood Clark, up to his waist in water. He reached out and pushed her to safety.

POMP

The flood had carried away the baby's basket. Holding him shivering and naked in her arms, with the cold rain pelting down on him, Sacajawea ran back to the boats. Clark followed. The only thing lost was his umbrella! When the danger was over, it did seem funny for an explorer to carry an umbrella into the wilderness. Still, he'd saved the life of his Indian guide and her baby.

Things like that were always happening. The trip was full of danger. As the explorers saw how calmly Sacajawea faced trouble and hardship, they liked her more and more. One trouble was the way her husband treated her. Sometimes he got angry and beat her.

Slowly the boats made their way up the river. Often Clark sat and played with the baby, whose father had named him Baptiste. But Clark called him Pomp. That was the name Sacajawea used. It was Shoshone for Leader. Clark named a great rock along the route Pomp's Tower in honor of Sacajawea's little son. Today people have forgotten how the rock got its name and they call it Pompey's Pillar.

Finally one day Sacajawea recognized the place where three creeks joined to form the Missouri River. Here was the exact spot where she had been taken prisoner.

"My people will be near by," she told Lewis and Clark joyfully, and from then on they kept a sharp lookout for Shoshones.

NEARING HOME

Soon Lewis saw an Indian in the distance. Quickly he took a blanket by two of its corners and waved it high over his head, then spread it on the ground. This was an Indian sign of friendship. But the Shoshone was suspicious of white men, and rode away.

Lewis hurried on ahead of the boats. Presently he met some Indian women who were out gathering roots. They were terrified, and sat down on the ground with their heads lowered. They were sure they were going to be killed, or at least taken captive. But Lewis put down his weapons and gave them presents. The women, reassured, led him to their camp. He was there when Sacajawea and the others arrived.

After her long wanderings, Sacajawea had come back. She put the tips of her fingers in her mouth—the sign-language way of saying that she recognized her own people. But more than that. She recognized a friend—a woman who had been captured with her, lived with her among the Hidatsas, and later escaped. The two of them hugged each other and did a little dance and laughed and cried for joy.

ONE WHO NEVER WALKS

Talking as fast as they could, the women walked toward the tepees. There Sacajawea had an even bigger surprise. Under the shelter of willow branches, Lewis was having a conference with the chief, who wore a beautiful ermine shawl and a band of otter skin around his head.

Lewis asked Sacajawea to come in. First she took off her moccasins at the entrance of the shelter. Shoshones always did this at a conference to show they were sincere about any agreements they made. It was a way of saying they would go barefoot on the jagged mountain paths the rest of their lives if they broke their word.

In the shelter Sacajawea sat down and began to say in Shoshone the things that Lewis and Clark asked her to say. But when the chief replied she stared at him, forgetting to translate. Suddenly she jumped up, ran over to him, gave him a big hug, and threw her robe around him as a sign of warmest greeting. The chief, Cameahwait—One Who Never Walks—was her own brother.

Now there were more important things than the white explorers and their trip. Sacajawea wanted her brother to try some wonderful new foods. She gave him a lump of sugar and some squash. He said they were the best things he'd ever tasted. She wanted to know about the rest of her family.

One of her sisters had died. So Sacajawea said she would adopt her sister's little boy, Bazil. He was too young to come along on the expedition, but Sacajawea said she would come back for him later. It turned out that adopting Bazil would be very important to Sacajawea in the future. Meantime, she and the other Shoshones had a wonderful time celebrating their reunion.

CHAPTER 7

The Great Journey

WHEN THE EXCITEMENT quieted down a little, the explorers and the Shoshones went on with their talks. Sacajawea translated and helped the white men and her own people to understand each other.

At last the bargaining was finished. Lewis and Clark had bought horses from the Indians. With her baby Baptiste in his basket on her back, Sacajawea rode away from the Muddy Water, up through the snowy passes of the Rocky Mountains. On the other side of the Continental Divide, she helped lead the explorers to the great Columbia River she had seen long ago.

As they floated down the Columbia in canoes, they began to meet new tribes whose ways seemed very strange to Sacajawea. The first were people called Flatheads—for the very simple reason that their heads were flat! It was fashionable here, west of the Rockies, to have a head shaped so that the line from the tip of the nose to the top of the head was straight. Mothers tied boards on the foreheads of their babies as they lay bundled up in wooden cradles. As the soft new bones grew they took the shape of the boards in long backward-slanting lines.

All the tribes along the Columbia had this strange custom, but the white men gave the name Flathead only to the first tribe they met.

Sacajawea discovered new ways of wearing decorations, too. Back on the plains, the Mandans hung big beads from their ears. Now she found people who put decorations in their noses. The first French traders who saw this tribe called it the Nez Percé (Pierced Nose).

Indians in the Northwest also had different ways of making their living. Besides gathering roots and berries that they dried and stored for winter, they fished a great deal. In summer the Columbia and the other rivers were full of large salmon, and the people built very clever traps in the water to catch them. They speared the big fish, too, and caught them with bone hooks. During the salmon season, everyone worked, catching and cleaning and drying and smoking the rich pink meat.

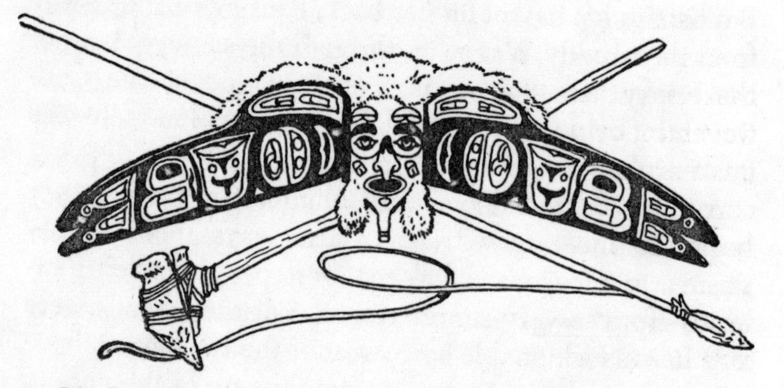

Mask and implements used by Pacific Coast Indians

Sacajawea was glad to have the fish. No buffalo lived here on the western side of the Rockies, and other game was scarce because there wasn't much grass.

HOUSES OF BOARDS

As she traveled from village to village down the river, Sacajawea found people living in wonderful big houses made of wide boards. To get the boards men built fires around the bases of huge red-cedar trees and then chopped away the charred wood with stone axes. Then when a tree fell down they split boards off the long trunk with hammers and wedges.

Inside, as well as outside, these houses were different from any she had ever seen. The floor was about four feet below the level of the ground and covered with woven mats. Along the walls ran bunks. Several fires—one for each family in the house—burned in a row down the center, and the smoke went out through an opening that ran the whole length of the roof. Inside hung fishing nets and great slabs of dried smoked salmon.

And these people wore hats! This was rainy country, so they kept their heads dry by wearing cone-shaped baskets on them. Some were very fancy with decorations woven in, or with an onion-shaped knob woven on top. Baskets were everywhere in the houses, filled with dried berry cakes, nuts, roots, and powdered dried salmon. Some tightly woven baskets could even hold water. There were boxes, too, that looked just like the ones the white explorers had—except that the boards were sewed together instead of nailed.

RICHES

The farther down the river Sacajawea floated in her skin canoe, the richer the people seemed to be. Everyone here had plenty of food, and they knew how to make all kinds of interesting things—blankets of mountain-goat hair, rain cloaks woven of shredded cedar bark, lots of decorations made from beautiful shells and beads, and canoes of many sizes hollowed out of cedar logs.

These rich Indians didn't hunt much, the way the Shoshones did, and they weren't farmers like the Hidatsas and the Mandans. But they did trade a great deal. All the Indians Sacajawea knew traded back and forth—sometimes getting things from great distances. But here trading was different. People were always looking for bargains—and they didn't like to give food away to anyone who needed it. They had plenty of everything, but they only gave if they got a bigger gift back, and then strangely complained that they had been cheated.

But strangest of all were the sights Sacajawea saw when she reached the Pacific Ocean. Here some of the cedar-log canoes were big enough to hold twenty or thirty men. They went far out on the huge water and were never tipped over by the waves. The ocean itself was a thing to marvel at. There always seemed to be food along the shore just waiting to be pulled out of the breakers or dug out of the sand.

A GIANT FISH

One day Sacajawea heard there was a giant fish on the shore seventeen miles away. She insisted on seeing it, and when she got there she found a giant creature sure enough. It stretched out for more than a hundred feet.

The Tillamook Indians who had caught the "fish"—which of course was a whale—cut off the blubber, and put it in boxes. Then they dropped hot stones into the boxes and boiled the oil out of the blubber. Later they stored the oil in bags made from the insides of the whale. Long afterward, when Sacajawea had come home and told her adventures, no one would believe she had seen such a big "fish." The Shoshones said she was fibbing!

Indians like these lived north of the Columbia River

Whale oil was a favorite food of the coast people. The Tillamooks and other tribes ate it with almost everything —even berries. And they ate the blubber like bacon after the oil had been boiled out of it. This one whale provided enough food to last a whole village for weeks, but still the Tillamooks wouldn't sell any of their oil or blubber unless they got a very good price for it. The payment they liked best of all was a particular kind of blue beads.

Many Coast Indians used these beads for money. Sacajawea herself had a belt made of them. One day Sacajawea gave up her belt so that Lewis and Clark could buy some beautiful sea-otter skins they wanted to show to President Jefferson as specimens. In return for the beads Lewis and Clark gave her a blue coat.

When the explorers reached the mouth of the Columbia River their westward journey was over. But they could not start right back across the Rockies. It was winter and the mountains were deep in snow. So they made a permanent camp. There Sacajawea set to work helping the men tan elk and deer skins and make moccasins and shirts and leggings. All the clothes they had started with were worn out.

BIG MEDICINE

Not long after they had settled down, there came a special day for everyone. Sacajawea didn't understand why the men were all celebrating and giving presents to each other and to her. She had never heard of Christmas. But the Shoshones and all other Indians she knew did have celebrations. "Big Medicine" days she called them. So on this Big Medicine day she gave a present to Clark, who loved to play with her baby. It was a gift that her people prized very highly—two white weasel, or ermine, skins. Giving was something she liked to do.

All winter long, Indian women came to see her. They even stayed overnight in her cabin. And she sometimes went to the villages that were close by. Always she found wonderful things to watch. The men were expert carpenters, working with only stone and bone tools and an occasional steel knife they had got from a trading vessel. They whittled spoons and bowls. They carved animals and human figures. (Farther north there were other fishing Indians who carved the history of their families on logs called totem poles.)

Sacajawea wondered at the skill of the men and at the deft fingers of the women as they turned heaps of dried grass and cedar bark into beautiful, useful baskets and hats. She watched them weave mats of rushes. The mats were both rugs on the floor and walls between families in the big barnlike wooden houses.

The first time Sacajawea saw the men's quivers, she thought they were very badly made. Instead of opening at the top, they had a hole where the arrows could be taken out at the side. Then she realized that these hunters never rode on horseback as Shoshones did. In fact, they seldom even hunted on foot. Instead, they shot their arrows as they knelt in canoes. So of course the side opening in the quiver was much more convenient.

When she visited her new neighbors, she borrowed a custom from them. She went barefoot. Klamath, Clatsop, Chinook, and other Coast Indians had no need for shoes on the sandy shore, even in winter. Back home Sacajawea had been glad for the winter moccasins of buffalo hide with the woolly hair left on the inside to keep her feet warm. But here there was no snow—only the heavy winter rains.

SLAVES

Sacajawea was so friendly and smiling that the women in all the different villages went out of their way to show her things. They talked in their languages and she talked in hers, and somehow they managed to understand each other with the help of gestures.

Then one day Sacajawea was amazed to hear good Shoshone words coming back in answer to a question! She found she was talking to one of her own people—a woman who, like herself, had been captured and made a slave among foreigners. All the Shoshone words that had been dammed up in Sacajawea burst out like a flood. She and the slave woman talked for hours and hours—about their memories of home and about all the strange ways of these rich West Coast people.

The Coast Indians were as rich in slaves as they were in everything else. But they were not nearly so friendly as her own people—or even the Hidatsas. When spring came, Sacajawea was glad enough to start back east, in spite of all the wealth and abundance around her. It was a good day indeed when she carried Baptiste to a canoe and the men started paddling up the Columbia.

Again they reached the high, snowy mountains. Now Lewis and Clark decided to take a different route from the one they had followed coming west. Sacajawea had never been here before, and she could not help find the way. For a while they were lost. Then they met some Chopunnisk (Nez Percé) Indians. Soon Sacajawea was asking for directions. This is how she got them:

First Lewis and Clark asked questions in English. Second, one of the other men translated the questions into French. Third, Charbonneau translated them into Hidatsa—the language in which he and Sacajawea talked to each other. Fourth, Sacajawea then asked the questions in Shoshone. Finally, a Shoshone boy who was a captive of the Chopunnisks translated the words into their language. Then the answers started back along the same route! It was a slow way of finding out how to get home, but it worked.

Sometimes the hunting was bad, and without Sacajawea the explorers would have gone hungry. She fed them with gooseberries and currants and roots, and with fennel, which tasted like licorice. The white men had never eaten fennel before, but after a while they got to like it very much.

All the way back, Clark played with the growing little brown-skinned boy Baptiste. But at last the time came to say good-by. The explorers reached the village where they'd first met Sacajawea. Clark proposed an idea he'd been thinking about. He wanted to take Baptiste along to St. Louis and send him to school.

Sacajawea smiled and said no, she wouldn't give Baptiste up. If he ever went to a white man's city, she would go, too. And she did, when Baptiste was old enough for school.

CHAPTER 8

More Travels

BAPTISTE was eight and a half years old. At last Sacajawea said the time had come for the trip to St. Louis. William Clark became Baptiste's guardian and sent him to school in the busy fur-trading town. Sacajawea lived there part of the time, too, because that was where her husband, Charbonneau, sold his furs.

St. Louis was a new adventure for Sacajawea. The white men had ways of living that were just as strange as the ways of the West Coast tribes had been. She learned to speak some of their English language. She saw how much better they could do some things than Indians could. And she saw their power. It was better to live at peace with these people than to fight them, she decided.

Baptiste, too, learned much in his school. Then when he was seventeen, he met a rich explorer from Germany. The German offered to take Baptiste to Europe for more education. Like his mother, Baptiste wanted to travel, and he agreed to go.

Meanwhile, Sacajawea had made up her mind to leave Charbonneau. She was tired of his beatings. The chance came one day when they met some Comanches on a fur-trading trip in Oklahoma. The Comanches were almost like her own Shoshone people. They spoke the same language. They had many of the same customs. Sacajawea was sure that she would find life among them better than it had been with Charbonneau. So she left his tepee, never to return.

Sacajawea felt at home in the constantly moving village of tepees. Soon she married a good hunter named Jerk Meat and started a new family.

The Comanches agreed with Sacajawea about one thing in particular. They wanted to keep peace with the whites. But at last they had to fight fiercely against the Texans, who had taken away their hunting grounds.

For years Sacajawea traveled and met strange new tribes in Oklahoma, Texas, New Mexico, and even as far west as Arizona. There she got to know the Apaches. She didn't like them, because they didn't share her ideas about peace. But she always explained that the Apaches were warlike because the white men had made them that way.

With every year that passed, the Comanches themselves had to fight more and more often to keep their lands. One day Sacajawea's husband was killed in battle. Now she began to feel lonely once more for her own people. Taking only her little daughter Crying Basket with her, she set out for the land of the Shoshones. On her way through Colorado she joined an exploring party led by General Frémont and traveled with him north along the edge of the Rocky Mountains.

At last she found her people in Wyoming, and once more there was a joyful reunion. Her son Baptiste had come back from Germany to live with the Shoshones!

Sacajawea's adopted son Bazil was there, too, and he had become an important chief. Although he had scarcely known her when he was a little boy, he considered her his mother. He lived in her tepee all the rest of her life and always loved her and cared for her.

By now Sacajawea was no longer young. She had traveled far and wide. She knew all the different parts of the West. She knew the ways of many different tribes—and the ways of white men. She was an important person. In fact, her people gave her a new name. They called her Porivo—Chief.

Soon she became the trusted adviser of Bazil and the great Chief Washakie. Together they always worked for peace with the white men. They made treaties, and got good reservation lands for the Shoshones.

Of all the things she had seen in her long years of wandering, one in particular seemed important to Sacajawea. She had watched the Hidatsas and the white people making food grow from the earth. Now she wanted her own people to become farmers. The buffalo were disappearing fast. Soon the Shoshones would need some other way to get food. Sacajawea set about helping them learn how to farm, and she kept on the best of terms with near-by Mormon settlers, who were expert farmers.

Although she was honored and a chief, Sacajawea still didn't lead a quiet life. She had traveled so much that she couldn't stop. She loved moving about, and people liked her so much that they made it easy for her to travel. White men who owned a stagecoach line gave her a free pass so that she could go wherever she wanted to.

Even the "bad men" in Wyoming liked the energetic brown woman who was always turning up in some unexpected place. One of the "bad men" happened to be a sheriff, too. He robbed stagecoaches at night and then hunted for the robbers during the day. So, when he saw Sacajawea getting into a coach one day, he tried to persuade her not to take this particular trip. She was stubborn. She wanted to go. But finally when the sheriff gave her three bags of flour, she agreed to stay at home. He didn't want her on that coach because he knew it was going to be robbed, and he was afraid the little old Indian woman might get hurt.

Many white people called Sacajawea Bird Woman instead of Boat Woman, which was the correct translation of her Indian name. The mistake had started long ago when Charbonneau carelessly made a wrong sign-language gesture in talking about her. The signs for Bird and Boat were very much alike. People thought Charbonneau had called her Bird Woman. Always after that there were arguments about her name, but the right one was Boat Woman.

With friends of every sort all around her, she lived till she was a hundred years old. Now there are monuments in many different places in honor of the brave young Shoshone mother who traveled with her baby on her back and helped Lewis and Clark explore a vast area of America.

(People tell the story of Sacajawea in different ways. I believe the way I have told it is true, although it isn't the same story you will find in some books.)

CHAPTER 9

The Talking Leaves

A SCRAP of a white man's newspaper fluttered across the field. At first the little man with a red turban on his head paid no attention to it. He had been up since dawn, when the village caller shouted, "He who expects to eat must work!" Now he was out looking for some lean, swift, half-wild pigs that had strayed away from home.

But suddenly the serious-faced Indian forgot his pigs —and his dignity. He ran after the scrap of paper as fast as his limping leg would take him. Here, he thought, might be the answer to a great question he had been asking himself. Although he did not understand a single word of the white men's language, he wanted a good look at the marks that white men made.

The little man's name was Sequoyah. Cherokee was the language that he and his people spoke. He was proud of his language and his people, and he had stubbornly refused to speak the strange English words. Sequoyah never did learn to read English—but, in the end, that bit of newspaper helped him make one of the most remarkable inventions that any one man ever made in the history of the world!

The Cherokees had a name for a page of writing. They called it a "talking leaf," because it was thin like a leaf, and because the white men could make the marks on it tell them things they wanted to remember. Sequoyah knew that this was important. Even more important, the leaves could carry thoughts and messages over great distances.

And so the question in Sequoyah's mind was this: How could he give his people talking leaves of their own?

FIRST EXPERIMENTS

The first time he ever saw white men scratching with their pens, he realized that they had some great power that the Cherokees did not have. Sequoyah began at once to scratch marks of his own on a stone. And he had been experimenting with all kinds of marks ever since. Now the piece of newspaper had given him some white men's writing to study. Perhaps it would help him find signs to use in writing down Cherokee words.

No matter where Sequoyah went, he experimented. With sharp pebbles he scratched on fence posts. He drew lines with charcoal on bark he peeled from trees. The walls of his log cabin were covered with marks.

Sometimes he talked with other Cherokees about what he was trying to do. But they laughed at him. The chiefs said he could never make a book. The Great Spirit, they said, had made a Cherokee boy and a white boy long, long ago. To the Cherokee boy he gave a book. To the white boy he gave a bow and arrow. But the white boy was not satisfied. He stole the book from the Cherokee and left the bow and arrow in its place. That was the way it had been ever since—the way it would always be.

Sequoyah knew what the chiefs meant. The white men were certainly powerful. Long ago the Cherokees had a huge, rich territory, all the way from Georgia up to Tennessee, where they farmed and hunted. But year after year the white men had claimed more and more of the Cherokees' land. Each time they took a chunk of land they said: "This is the last one. From now on the rest of your lands are yours forever." This had happened every four or five years since Sequoyah was a little boy.

And now the white men had made a new demand. They said the Cherokees must leave their territory and move far west beyond the frontier to Arkansas.

The Cherokees had very good reasons for not wanting to move. Their farms were rich and well cared-for. They were just as settled in their villages as any white people were. In the beginning, it was they who had taught white men how to raise tobacco and corn. Now the Cherokees had learned from the newcomers how to be even better farmers than they had been in the past.

Iron hoes and shovels made their work easier. Instead of hunting, the Cherokees raised tens of thousands of cattle and pigs. Horses pulled their plows or the wagons that carried corn to mills owned by the tribe. They had blacksmith shops where tools were made and repaired. They had cotton gins and ferries and sawmills.

TURBANS FOR INDIANS

Hundreds and hundreds of Cherokee women owned spinning wheels. They wove cloth for the red-fringed jackets and leggings. And they wove the shawls that men like Sequoyah wound into turbans around their heads.

There was an interesting story about those turbans. They had been fashionable for about three hundred years—ever since the first white traders came to the South. The traders brought the turbans because they had heard that Columbus had discovered the East Indies, or

India. Of course everybody knew that people in India wore turbans! The traders soon found that they'd made a mistake in geography, but not in the goods they carried. They started a new fad for turbans. So it was that this tribe of American Indians actually dressed a little like the Indians of Asia, for whom they had been named.

The Cherokees had been quick to adopt other ideas, and now they were just as prosperous as white farmers near by. The only difference was that they had their own customs and beliefs and spoke their own language.

All of this sounds very good. But to the white people it seemed very bad! They didn't like it when the proud and independent Cherokees said, "We are a separate nation, living in our own country." And so, time and again, the Cherokees were forced to sign treaties giving some of their land away.

TO MAKE THEM STRONG

It was no wonder that the Cherokees had little faith in such things as "talking leaves." But Sequoyah looked at things differently. He felt sure that reading and writing would help to hold his people together and make them strong. So he kept stubbornly at work.

Daytimes Sequoyah's mind wandered to his writing, and he forgot to hoe the corn. At night he worked in his cabin by the light of a burning pine knot. The light was poor, and Sequoyah found he had to get spectacles.

Slowly the quiet, inquisitive little man invented a thousand pictures or signs for a thousand different words in the Cherokee language. But the job seemed endless. Who could remember a thousand signs? And he had only started.

By this time, Sequoyah's wife had a thousand complaints. She didn't see the need for sitting all day and all night making marks while she did the farm work and the housework, too. At last she couldn't stand it any longer. She tossed all of Sequoyah's talking leaves into the fire.

All this time the United States Government had been trying to make the Cherokees move. Finally Sequoyah saw that his people would have to give in. He joined a group that set out for the West in flatboats. They floated first down the Tennessee River to the Mississippi, then on down to Arkansas. At last they settled in the wilderness, a hundred and fifty miles farther west.

Now the Cherokee tribe was divided. Part was in Arkansas, but a large part still remained way back East. If Sequoyah could only invent some kind of writing, the two groups could talk to each other across the distance.

CHAPTER 10

Sequoyah's Success

IN THE ARKANSAS WILDERNESS Sequoyah started a new farm with a new log cabin. Perhaps his wife thought he had given up his queer ideas about talking leaves. But he hadn't. He built himself a little shack where nobody would bother him. And there he scribbled on in peace.

The only person who took any interest in his strange marks was his six-year-old daughter. She visited his shack often. And her constant chatter was actually a great help to him. Listening to the little girl one day, Sequoyah found a simple way to solve his great problem. All of a sudden, after twelve long years of study, he knew exactly what to do! The idea was so simple that it doesn't even seem like a great invention. And yet it was.

Sequoyah discovered that his language was made up of groups of sounds or syllables that occur over and over again in different combinations. In English there are syllables, too. For instance, the word "buffalo" has three of them–*buff-a-lo*. We use six different letters to write the word. But if we had a sign standing for each syllable, it could be written with only three signs. Sequoyah realized that all he needed to do was to make a sign for each different syllable.

He worked feverishly for a month. He listened to the Cherokee language in a new way, noticing all the sounds and separating them into syllables. At last he found that he could make all the Cherokee words by using 86 different syllables in different combinations.

This is where that scrap of newspaper came in—the scrap he had found so long ago when he was out looking for his pigs. Sequoyah copied all the letters he found in the newspaper and assigned new jobs to them. He decided that each letter would stand for a whole Cherokee syllable. He didn't know what the letters stood for in English, and he didn't care. For example, he made the letter *k* stand for the Cherokee syllable *tso.*

THE NEW ALPHABET

Of course there weren't enough English letters to go round. So Sequoyah made up enough more to fill out the whole list of 86 that he needed. Now, by putting down the signs in the right combinations, he could write anything he wanted in the Cherokee language.

Sequoyah and his daughter tried his invention out. It worked. In no time at all the little girl had learned how to read and write!

Very soon one of Sequoyah's sons had learned, too. The signs were so simple and easy that anyone could be reading and writing in three or four days—instead of spending years, as white children have to do.

But still people laughed when Sequoyah told them of his great invention. No one would believe in his talking leaves. His friends thought he was crazy.

"All right," Sequoyah said quietly, "I'll show you." Before the eyes of the chiefs and other members of the tribe, he sat down with a piece of bark and a pen he had made from a feather, the way he had seen white men do. Then he sent his son to wait at a distance. The chiefs told Sequoyah what to write on the bark, and they made sure that the boy couldn't possibly hear what they were saying.

Bending his turbaned head over the bark, Sequoyah solemnly scratched away with his pen. Then he handed the bark to one of the chiefs. The whole group walked over to the boy, still making sure that Sequoyah could not signal to his son in any way. To their utter amazement, the boy looked at the bark and told them exactly what the chiefs had asked his father to write down. Sequoyah wasn't crazy after all!

THE NATION AT SCHOOL

A buzz of excitement went through the crowd. Now everyone wanted to try Sequoyah's trick. Within four days, all the Cherokees who saw the experiment had learned the new magic of the talking leaves. They sent messages to each other on bark. They wrote stories on cabin walls. They carved news into the trunks of trees. The Cherokee people in Arkansas felt closer together than they had ever felt before.

Soon the chiefs made up a message to send from their new home in Arkansas to the Cherokees who still remained in the East. Sequoyah set out with the message on the long journey back to Georgia.

There the excitement about his invention spread. The whole Cherokee nation suddenly found itself going to school. After Sequoyah had taught the Eastern people to read and write, he returned with a message to Arkansas. At last he was happy. He had brought the two distant parts of his tribe together.

Before long, the Cherokees in the East raised enough

money to buy a printing press and to have special Cherokee type made. In 1827 they published the first issue of their newspaper, the *Cherokee Phoenix*. Soon they wrote a very democratic constitution for their independent nation and printed it in the paper for all to study.

Nobody laughed at quiet, patient little Sequoyah now. His tribe honored him and gave him a silver medal. They held a great feast for him. And wherever he went he was listened to as the wisest of wise men. He even traveled to Washington, where famous white people wanted to meet him and learn how one man could invent writing.

ANOTHER TREATY

At the same time other white men kept on trying to squeeze the Cherokee people out of their new rich farming lands in Arkansas. In the end, the chiefs had to sign another treaty saying that their tribe would move on to Oklahoma.

Although they were ashamed at having to sign the treaty, the chiefs were proud that now they could write their names in their own language, instead of just putting down a cross mark the way they had always done before.

Because Sequoyah was so loved and honored, the chiefs insisted on a special paragraph about him in the treaty. The United States Government had to promise that it would pay him five hundred dollars as a gift for his great service to his people. The treaty also provided that the Government would give the Cherokees money for a new printing press. Their old one had been taken over by white people, who used it to persuade the Eastern Cherokees to move away, too.

The Government never paid Sequoyah all the money

that had been agreed on, and it never gave the Cherokees their new printing press. But the chiefs had done their best to reward Sequoyah for his talking leaves.

THE TRAIL OF TEARS

Once more the Cherokees moved on. The group from Arkansas reached Oklahoma first and settled on the best of the land that had been assigned to the tribe. Then seventeen thousand started out from the East, herded along by Regular Army troops. By the time they reached Oklahoma, 4000 of the Cherokees had died of hunger and disease on what they called the Trail of Tears.

At the journey's end, they found all of the best land taken by their fellow tribesmen from Arkansas. This was more than they could stand. Trouble between the Eastern and Western Cherokees started. Once again Sequoyah acted to bring all his people closer together in peace. He helped settle the quarrels and get justice for all, under a new constitution. He even prevented a war between the Oklahoma Cherokees and a group who had settled in Texas. Finally, he persuaded the Texas group to join the tribe in Oklahoma and settle there. Unity and peace for his people were the great things he always sought.

SILVERSMITH, PAINTER, TEACHER

Meantime Sequoyah's clever hands found other things to do besides writing. Without any teacher, he learned to be an expert silversmith. Taking silver he got from white traders, he made beautiful spurs for Cherokee men to use as they rode their horses. He made silver spoons and decorations, too. Sequoyah was an artist with silver, and a painter as well. He made his own brushes from the hairs of wild animals. These brushes were actually another one of his inventions. Sequoyah had never seen a white man's brush.

Horses and buffalo were the things he liked best to paint. People who saw his work said that no man in the United States could draw a buffalo better than this small, lame Indian who still wore a homespun shirt with red fringe and a red turban on his head.

In Oklahoma, near the town of Sallisaw, Sequoyah had a farm with several mules and cows and three cabins. Often he made extra money by selling salt that he made from the water of a salt spring. Even as he worked, boiling the spring water down into salt, Sequoyah kept on teaching people about his magic talking leaves.

It seemed there were always new things to teach—and to learn. He wasn't satisfied with just reading and writing. He made up signs for numbers, too. He figured out arithmetic all by himself and taught that to his people. He was such a good teacher that the Cherokees built a schoolhouse for him. Students went there for regular classes to learn all Sequoyah could tell them.

HEROIC MISSION

The little man grew older, but he never forgot his dream of uniting all the Cherokees into a real nation that would be peaceful and prosperous. When he was over seventy (nobody is quite sure how old he was, because nobody knows exactly when he was born), Sequoyah kept thinking of a story he had heard. According to the tale, a band of Cherokees had gone to live in

Mexico. Quietly he planned with a small group of friends to set out in search of the Mexican Cherokees.

Sequoyah knew that people would object to his going. They would say he was too old and frail. They would say he was too lame for such a long journey. Sequoyah knew he was getting old. That was why he wanted to make the trip now. He must go to Mexico before it was too late. As for his lameness, he had always limped, but that hadn't ever kept him from doing the important things he wanted to do.

So he set out with his friends for Mexico. On the way he got sick, but he kept on. Exploring in strange country where there were no roads and no people who spoke his language, he pushed farther and farther toward the south.

Finally he found that the story he had heard was true. A band of Cherokees did live in Mexico. But Sequoyah died before he could succeed in this last effort to bring all his people together.

Sequoyah was never a chief himself, but he was loved and respected by everyone in his tribe, including the chiefs. Even beyond the tribe, people recognized his greatness, and his name lives on today. The gigantic redwood trees in California are called *sequoias* in his honor. At his home in Sallisaw, the Cherokees have built a stone building over his log cabin to protect it and to make it into a monument. That is one way of saying: Here lived a man whom the 40,000 Cherokees who now live in Oklahoma want to remember always.

CHAPTER 11

First American Pioneers

SHARP SHINS and Sitting Bull, Sacajawea and Sequoyah, were all real Indians who lived in this country after the white men arrived. But their ancestors had lived here for thousands of years.

The ancient Indians didn't write their history down in words, but they did leave records of another kind that experts can read today. Old camp sites and burial grounds, lost arrows and pots and tools—all these give facts and clues to the men who dig them up and study them. Here is the story told by scientific detectives:

Twenty-five thousand or more years ago there were no people at all on the two huge American continents, but hunters did roam over Europe and Asia. At that time the great glaciers of the Ice Age were melting and leaving the earth bare so that food for men and animals could grow again. Near the edges of the glaciers were moss and lichen that the caribou liked to eat. As the ice melted back farther and farther, the caribou followed. And hunters followed the caribou.

At last one band of Asian hunters reached the very northeastern tip of Siberia. Today a stretch of water fifty miles wide separates Siberia from Alaska. The chances are that the distance was much less when those ancient hunters arrived. Perhaps there was even land all the way from Siberia to Alaska. Much of the earth's water was still frozen into glaciers at the North of the world, and that meant the level of the ocean was lower.

At any rate, it wasn't hard to get from Asia to America. (It isn't hard even now. Today Eskimos in Siberia and Alaska visit back and forth across the Bering Strait in their little skin boats.) And so that first band of hunters crossed over from Asia to America, searching for food. The farther they went, the greater was their wonder and surprise. In Alaska they saw as many animals in a day as they'd seen in a week on the cold Siberian plains. The climate on the coast was much warmer. What's more, there was not a single human being in all the vast land ahead of them.

A MOUNTAIN OF MEAT

In the years that followed, more bands of hunters crossed to the rich new land. These immigrants all had dark skins and black hair. Some were tall, with long, narrow heads. Others were short and chunky and had round heads. They came in all sizes and shapes, and they spoke different languages. But they all adventured into the unknown searching for more food and easier lives.

Once they had reached their new land, the wanderers kept on wandering. Year after year they pushed on farther, until at last they came to the very southernmost point in South America—Tierra del Fuego.

Although these people lived so many thousands of years ago, we know for certain what some of their adventures were and what strange sights they saw along their way. Large camels roamed the country in those days, and so did giant bison, much larger than buffalo.

Giant sloths ambled along with their paws doubled under so that all their toes turned up backward. Tiny three-toed horses raced over the great open plains.

One day the earliest hunters caught a glimpse of a creature so huge they could scarcely believe it was real. No man would dare to hunt it by himself. But, working together, the men tricked the enormous mastodon into a swamp and killed it with their sharp stone-pointed spears. Using their brains—the best weapon of all—they brought down a whole mountain of meat.

All these giant animals have disappeared now. Some scientists believe that the ancient hunters were so successful in trapping the great beasts that they killed them all off. The camels and bison and sloths are gone, too. Even the tiny horses died out, leaving two whole continents without any strong beast of burden for men to use.

DIFFERENT PLACES—DIFFERENT CUSTOMS

Groups of hunters kept moving southward through the mountains. Along the way, some of them dropped out. The hunting was good enough for them where they were. But they, too, kept changing their ways of doing things as they found new foods and new materials.

They invented new ways of shaping stone into tools. They chipped flint into spearheads and knives. They experimented with animal bones and found that they could make punches for leather and fine needles.

Ten thousand or more years went by, and still the hunters wandered. Some groups had their camps along the eastern side of the Rocky Mountains. Scientists call these people Folsom men, because the first traces of their ancient hunting camps were found near the town

Early Indians hunted buffalo with spears

of Folsom in New Mexico. The tools and bones and decorations of these early Indians lay buried in the earth for at least 15,000 years before they were discovered!

The Folsom men lived along one of the main routes that hunters followed between Alaska and South America. This route ran up the Yukon and Mackenzie rivers, then down the eastern edge of the Rocky Mountains. Another main route ran along the southern shore of Alaska, then inland along the Columbia River, and from there down south between the Rocky Mountains and the Sierra Nevadas, through Utah, Nevada, and Arizona.

You may think that this part of the country was too dry and barren for hunting. But when the first Indians came, they found great lakes where there is only desert now. The land around the lakes was rich and green, and there was plenty of game.

By these two main routes, and probably by hundreds of crisscross trails, the wanderers kept pushing steadily southward. In those days, no Indians had learned how to farm. They had not even discovered that they could weave baskets or shape cooking pots from clay. They just hunted and moved their simple skin tents from one hunting ground to another, traveling always on foot. But they had much better spear points and knives than the first pioneer Indians brought with them from Siberia. They had made progress.

Then, all of a sudden, a group that had reached Central or South America made an amazing discovery—one of the great discoveries of the world.

CHAPTER 12

An Amazing Invention

ONE HOT DAY more than five thousand years ago, a band of Indians near the Equator found a new kind of grass. It was tall, and it had seed pods about the size and shape of a small pine cone. Inside the pods grew little sharp-pointed seeds, each one wrapped in a husk of its own. When the seeds were cooked, they made good food.

The Indians decided to stay awhile in the river valley where the tall grass grew. The women gathered many of the pods and husked them in their camp. After a while they noticed that new shoots of the pod-bearing grass were coming up in the spot where they had taken the husks from the seeds. Could it be that seeds turned into grass?

The women decided to find out. They covered some seeds with earth and watched. Sure enough, grass came up. This was a wonderful discovery. Now they could make things grow, instead of just gathering food where they happened to find it.

Perhaps you've guessed what the big grass was. It was the ancestor of corn. But it didn't look like our corn. The pod was really a cluster of seeds that grew on a tiny cob. Each kernel had its own wrapping. Our corn has bare kernels on the cob, and one husk wraps around them all.

It was the Indians who changed this early corn and *made* it grow a single wrapping outside all the kernels.

We are used to the idea that scientists can change plants. But long ago, before plant science was ever heard of, those first Indian farmers did an amazing thing: They developed a new kind of grass from an old kind. It must have happened something like this:

ONE EQUALS THREE HUNDRED

Every once in a while the women found a cob that had a bare kernel or two, protected by the husks of the kernels around it. Pods like these were valuable, because there were fewer tiresome husks to take off.

The women saved the bare seeds and planted them year after year. Gradually the plants changed. At last the women had a whole crop of corn that grew in ears much like our corn—ears with all the kernels bare and the whole thing wrapped in an outside husk.

At the same time, other improvements were going on. The Indians discovered they could grow bigger kernels if they saved the biggest seeds. They could grow more kernels if they saved seeds from the ears that had the most.

Before long this marvelous discovery would change the lives of Indians in most parts of North and South America. Later on, it would give better lives to billions of people over the whole world. Here was a plant that could grow three hundred new seeds from one seed planted in the ground. The best wheat grew only twenty or thirty new kernels from one. But first, news of the discovery had to spread.

The discoverers of corn gave up their wandering and settled down around their fields. They didn't need to travel in search of food any longer. But they sometimes visited other tribes, and others visited them. Soon they were trading their precious corn seed for sea shells and tools and various other things they wanted.

This trading of seed went on from one tribe to another. Corn spread to Peru on the west side of the Andes Mountains. It spread north until many different parts of North America knew about it. And as it traveled, Indians kept on making experiments with it. They found that seeds which grew well in one place grew poorly in another. But always there were a few seeds that lived in a new place, and from them people developed different varieties of corn that flourished in different climates.

When the wandering seeds reached Mexico, Indians did another exciting thing. They changed the shape of the cobs and they put more kernels on each ear. This they did by crossing corn with a wild grass called *teosinte*. After a while the brand-new kind of corn spread all over the two Americas.

But meantime the older kind had wandered on beyond Mexico. Indian traders carried it farther and farther north. One day they met some hunters at just about the place where the four corners of New Mexico, Colorado, Utah, and Arizona now meet. The hunters liked the corn food that the traders offered them. Before long they had their own fields. Corn had completely changed their lives. Instead of roaming, they settled down in one place and started a wonderful history that led up to the Pueblo Indians, who still live near the Four Corners region today.

CHAPTER 13

Basket Makers

POLLEN GIRL ran her fingers through her very short hair and walked toward the edge of the mesa—a high flat plain on top of a mountain. Deep canyons cut into the mountainside, with cliff walls as steep as if they had been carved by a giant knife. Here in this strange-looking and beautiful place that we call Mesa Verde, Pollen Girl's people had settled down to farm. Other similar groups were farming all over a big area of the Southwest.

Looking into the canyon bottom below, Pollen Girl could see corn patches spread out. Behind her, on top of the mesa, more fields pushed back the gnarled piñon pines and juniper trees. At this moment none of the men were working in the fields. They had all gone to hold a ceremony in one of their homes.

The houses in Pollen Girl's village were roughly circular, built partly below ground in pits, and with roofs of poles and adobe mud above the ground. The entrance to a pit house was through the smoke hole in the roof.

Years before, Pollen Girl's ancestors had started digging pits as storage places for their food. Then they discovered that their storehouses could be enlarged and changed into places in which to live. Year after year the men found better ways of making the pole roofs and bracing them securely. They built in ventilators—chimneys at one side, not to let smoke out but to let fresh air in. Now families could squat around the fire at the center of the room, beneath the smoke hole, without being blinded and choked up by smoke. And of course the ventilator invention made the houses more comfortable for the men when they danced in their ceremonies.

The women had kept on doing things in new ways too. As crops from the farms increased they needed more and better baskets in which to store their corn and dried squash and beans. They borrowed new styles for their baskets from those in which traders from the south often carried their goods. But, of course, the women used the material that they found close by. They shredded the shaggy bark of juniper trees and wove the fibers together. They learned that they could take the long, spiky leaves of yucca plants, pound them, and soak them till nothing was left but fibers that made the best baskets of all. They invented new stitches, and even learned to weave the strands so tightly that the baskets held water.

As Pollen Girl stood at the cliff edge, she saw her mother climbing the steep path from the canyon, carrying a load of water from the spring below. Behind her came a trader and his helpers loaded down with goods.

Soon all the women of the village gathered around. The trader, who spoke a strange language, pointed to the damp water basket. Then he opened one of his packs and took out a pot that was made of clay but shaped like a basket. Stooping quickly, he poured some water into the pot. Not a drop leaked through!

The women were excited and amazed. Then the trader carried the pot to the cooking fire, and in no time the water was boiling—a greater wonder still. Always before they had heated water by dropping hot stones into a water basket. The women began to bargain. In exchange for the pot they gave the trader robes woven from strips of rabbit skin, sandals of yucca fiber and strong cord made from their own hair.

After the stranger left, the women started to make pots of their own by covering baskets with clay, or by lining them with clay and then letting them dry in the sun. But something was wrong with this experiment. The pots did not hold water very well, and they chipped and cracked easily. At last someone discovered that the clay had to be mixed with crushed rock or sand and then baked in a hot fire. Pots made in this way were strong and they held water.

Pollen Girl learned these things, and from now on all her life she experimented with pottery. After a while she managed to shape the clay all by itself, without the basket for a mold. Now some of the long hours of basket weaving were over. A small pot took only half an hour to make, and the biggest ones could be finished in five hours.

Any timesaver was welcome, because women had many jobs to do. One in particular took Pollen Girl several hours each day—the task of grinding corn by hand. First she put the whole kernels on a big stone slab that was slightly hollowed out in the middle. Then, kneeling, she rubbed a smaller stone back and forth over the corn to break it up.

All this rubbing gradually wore the sandstone away, and there was always some grit in the corncakes. People were used to gritty bread, but it wasn't good for them. Their teeth wore away. By the time they were thirty years old they had almost no teeth left. (Scientists have figured out that a member of the village chewed up in his lifetime all the sand from two of the big grinding stones!)

DOGS FOR WOOL

In the fall, Pollen Girl went with the other women to gather piñon nuts and yucca pods to eat and yucca roots to use as soap. Those who had small babies carried them wrapped snugly and strapped to cradle boards. At home, they propped the cradles up in the yard, and the babies could be amused by watching the dogs and the tame turkeys scratching for food.

Turkeys and dogs were useful pets, but Pollen Girl never had tasted a turkey dinner. She raised the birds only for their feathers. The men used the biggest feathers in their ceremonies down in the kiva, and they wove the small ones into soft warm robes and blankets.

The dogs were kept the way people keep sheep—for their hair! Men sheared them and wove the wool into cloth for breechcloths and handsome decorated belts.

Dog-wool cloth and yucca-fiber cloth were the only ones that Pollen Girl knew until a man from her village came home after a trading trip far to the south. With him he brought a new kind of seed—cotton seed. The plants grew well in the fields, and cotton provided fine, soft cloth. It changed the fashion in women's hair-do's too. Cotton could be twisted into strong cords. Instead of cutting their hair to make it into cord, the women could let it grow long. From now on they wore it coiled into a knot over each ear.

All her life Pollen Girl delighted in trying new things and in experimenting with familiar things around her.

By the time her grandson, Juniper Boy, was half-grown, life had become much easier for people in the village on the mesa. Then something happened that brought a great change.

Pueblo pottery

CHAPTER 14

Farmers in the Cliffs

JUNIPER BOY stared at a clump of brush along the edge of the cornfield. He thought he saw something moving—something bigger than a rabbit. Perhaps it was a deer. Moving silently on his sandaled feet, he left the other men and boys and went toward the bushes. Then, to his utter amazement, a strange-looking man stepped out, dropped some curious things he had in his hand, and made a sign of friendship.

Juniper Boy couldn't understand a word the man said, so he called out to the others in the field. He couldn't make any sense, either, of the strange things the man had dropped on the ground—a long curved stick with a leather thong attached, and some tiny little spears that looked like toys.

None of Juniper Boy's people had ever seen a bow and arrows before. They handled them curiously and asked with gestures what they were for.

The visitor took an arrow, fitted it against the thong, and looked around. Down the field a rabbit had come out of hiding. Suddenly the stranger let his arrow fly and ran after it. In a few moments he was back with the rabbit, and Juniper Boy saw that the little spear had flown straight through the air to its distant target. No man he knew could throw a big spear that accurately and that far.

Here was something new and wonderful. Everyone

wanted to know more about it. The stranger stayed and showed them how to make bows and arrows of their own. Then friends of the stranger came from the south. They settled down on the mesas and soon the two groups were one.

Gradually the mesa people worked out ways of improving their homes. They began to build them of stone, entirely above ground. But they kept on using the pit houses for ceremonies. As their homes moved above ground, the pit houses moved farther and farther underground. There, in complete secrecy, the men of the village met and worked magic around a fire. They danced to the sound of drums and sang songs to the Rain Spirit or the Corn Spirits or other spirits they believed were important.

The men's dances and ceremonies were part fun and part serious—somewhat like a combination of movies and church. The men enjoyed them, but they also thought the things they did were very useful indeed.

(More than a thousand years have gone by since that time, but Indians in the Four Corners region still have these same secret ceremonial rooms, which they call kivas.)

Juniper Boy lived to see some of these new-fashioned stone houses and underground kivas being built. By the time his great-grandchildren were growing up, the people of the mesas had mingled more and more with the southerners who had introduced them to bows and arrows. They were becoming part of a group we now call Pueblo Indians.

As the years went by, they still welcomed new ideas and the visitors who brought them. But at last their friendliness caused them great trouble. New tribes began to move into the area, tribes who knew nothing about farming. When the hunting was bad, the strangers simply raided the farmers' villages and stole corn.

Such a thing had never bothered the Mesa Verde people much before. The hunting tribes caught them by surprise and robbed them easily.

This was the beginning of a bad time. Year after year the hunters raided. The villagers fought back with the bows and arrows they had learned how to make and use. They even built tall watchtowers that were also forts. But still the wild warriors managed to steal much of their corn. Something had to be done.

A group of women, carrying pots of water on their heads from a spring at the bottom of a canyon, had the startling new idea that solved the problem. Just above the spring there was a big cave in the sheer stone wall. If they could take shelter there, they would be safe.

The women talked with the men, and the men began to explore. They found they could climb up to the cave. With their stone hammers they chipped out steps and handholds in the rather soft rock of the cliff wall. In places that were too steep, they placed ladders that could be drawn up to keep the enemy out.

Everyone agreed it was safer to move into the cave and live there all the time. They would still be close enough to water and to their fields and cotton.

So they got to work. They even moved their houses, carrying them stone by stone up into the cave. In order to have shelter for everyone, they had to put one house on top of another, with ladders to the upper stories, and sometimes with little balcony platforms out in front.

The mesa's people had become good masons. They built their new stone houses solidly, three and four and even five stories high. The rooms were so tiny that there was no way to cook in them, as there had been in the houses on the mesa. So all the families built fires in the flat courtyard in front of the apartment buildings they had set up. Otherwise they went on living as they had out in the open.

Other villagers in the mesa country seized the new idea and built their own cliff dwellings. Before long there were scores of apartment houses in the caves.

Now people in the cliffs had to learn some new ways of doing things. As soon as they could walk, the children had to remember to keep away from the cliff edge at the front of the cave. Boys and girls learned to climb up and down, using the footholds and handholds or the ladders, which sometimes had rungs and sometimes were made simply of notched logs. After a while almost everybody grew wonderfully skillful at carrying loads over the dangerous routes to the caves. Still, there were accidents sometimes, and broken bones had to be nursed.

Babies still rode on cradle boards, up and down the cliffs. But now a new fashion swept through the villages. Mothers bound their babies' heads tightly against the cradle boards to make them very flat at the back.

Other fashions changed, too, as people found time to think about such things. They painted designs on the walls of rooms. They put handsome decorations on pottery. They even made their corn beautiful. Along with other Indian neighbors, they planted many new varieties and colors—blue, pink, speckled, dark purple, white. When the women spread the husked ears out to dry on the roofs of the cliff dwellings, the whole village looked like a brilliant flower garden. They cooked the corn in many different ways, too. They even had popcorn.

More and more turkeys now ran all over the courtyards

Juniper Boy chased the turkeys in front of his cliff house

in front of the cliff dwellings, and over the refuse dump below. Turkeys were becoming more valuable as people invented new things to do with their feathers. The men sometimes made leggings for winter out of turkey-feather cloth. Occasionally they had turkey meat to eat.

All this rich life invited enemies, and the cliff dwellers had to watch out. They made the entrances to the courtyards so cleverly that no big raiding party could force its way through narrow guarded passageways.

But friendly visitors were still welcome. A trader from Mexico brought a brilliant green parrot and exchanged it for the delicately shaped sky-blue turquoise beads made in the caves. Pawnee Indians from the Great Plains traded dried buffalo meat for feather blankets, and they marveled at the tools the cliff dwellers had invented—chisels and fine drills and especially a kind of wrench for straightening the gnarled branches into perfect arrows.

Down in the canyon bottoms, newly built dams saved up water from the rare rains. Irrigation ditches and terraced fields helped to produce better crops.

Still, there were many things the cliff dwellers did not know. And, like most Indians, they thought that spirits caused troubles they could not understand. As their farms prospered, the men had more free time. They used much of it for ceremonies they hoped would please the spirits.

Some of the new ceremonies were borrowed from Indians far to the south. Others came from farming villages that dotted the country near by and were very like the villages in the cliffs. And of course there were still the beloved old dances that had been handed down from their ancestors, the Basket Makers.

The cliff dwellings, which seemed so far away from the rest of the world, were really part of a great melting pot in the Southwest where ideas and inventions from many places were stirred together and made into something new.

For two hundred years, life on the steep canyon walls grew richer and more gay. Here people were peaceful and free and independent, with no lords or kings to order them about. Working all together, they had found a way of making more wealth for everyone. Then came disaster.

ANGRY RAIN GODS

Trouble started when several years went by with very little rain. The cliff dwellers thought they were having a drought because they hadn't pleased the gods.

So people from all the villages began working together on a plan they hoped would bring better times. They decided to build a new place for ceremonies out on the open mesa—a place so great that surely the gods would be pleased and rain would fall once again.

Children were hungry as they helped carry stones for the temple walls. Although the women spent all day looking, they could find scarcely any berries or seeds or piñon nuts. The grass had died and hunters brought home few rabbits. Work on the great building went slowly because people were weak from lack of food.

You would say that the temple was a strange-looking place, because it didn't have a single door in the outside walls. Most of the rooms inside didn't, either. The building was planned with entrances through the roof. If fierce raiders came, the temple would be a fortress too. With no doors to guard, the cliff dwellers would only need to pull up their ladders and they would be safe.

But the great building was never finished. The drought, which began in the year 1276, lasted until 1299. For twenty-four years no rain fell. Beans and pumpkins shriveled. Even the trees stopped growing.

Day after day, week after week, the men gathered in the kivas, hoping for guidance from the spirits.

At last one man proposed a plan. He had been on long

A city and farm in the cliffs

trading trips toward the Gulf of Mexico, and he had seen a river whose waters never dried up. Why not move to the river, where there were friendly people who lived in villages and farmed just as people in the cliffs did?

His family and a few others packed up their most precious belongings. The trip would be too long and hard for heavy packs. One morning they set off down the canyon, looking sadly back at the beautiful cliff-dwelling homes, which were still filled with pots and blankets, heavy grinding stones and toys and pretty yucca mats.

Many other families followed. Finally all of them came. Moving south and east, they reached the Rio Grande River, which was fed by melting snows on distant peaks. Water at last!

Near the river stood villages where Indian farmers lived. The weary travelers were delighted at the houses. They were very much like their own cliff dwellings! Families in the river village built their homes all together, piling them on top of each other, several stories high. But instead of using stone, they made the walls of sundried adobe (clay) blocks.

The farmers were friendly. They offered the starving pilgrims good fresh corn bread and delicious stewed squash. Children, and parents too, gobbled the banquet spread out before them. They were so hungry it didn't matter that some of the food tasted unfamiliar.

Now the cliff dwellers asked if they might have fields for themselves along the river. There was plenty of land, so they were allowed to settle down near by. Once more they made farms that were rich and good.

CHAPTER 15

The Seven Cities of Cibola

THE CLIFF DWELLERS had settled down in their new homes a long time before Columbus discovered the Arawaks and called them Indians. For almost two hundred years the Pueblo Indians—new ones as well as old ones—lived peacefully, except when Navahos and Apaches raided their villages.

Then, in 1540, the Spanish conqueror Coronado came from Mexico with his soldiers. He had heard that somewhere along the Rio Grande River was a fabulous place called the Seven Cities of Cibola, each city rich in gold.

The Seven Cities turned out to be a dusty disappointment for Coronado and his men. They were only pueblos built of adobe mud, with no gold in them at all. But there *was* food.

Coronado had his heart set on gold, and he took food from the Pueblos for his men to eat while they kept hunting treasure all over the Southwest.

For two long years the terrified Indians watched the white men come and go. They had never seen horses before, and it was always frightening to watch the big animals, with men on their backs, running as fast as deer. The white men wore a kind of hard, shiny clothes they called armor, through which no arrow could pierce. And they did not come as friends.

The Indians found ways of killing some of the men

who stole their corn. Then many of the Spaniards, including Coronado himself, sickened and died in the desert country, where they did not know how to live. The rest, disgusted because they still had not found gold, returned to the Spanish settlements in Mexico.

THE CONQUERORS RETURN

The Indians rejoiced when the Spaniards disappeared. But their happiness did not last long. The white men took with them the knowledge that the Pueblo country was rich in food, with grazing land enough for numberless herds of cattle and flocks of sheep. And after fifty years they came back. With them they brought not only cattle and sheep but also many burros and horses.

This time the Spaniards had no intention of hunting for gold. They were looking for wealth of another kind, which they knew they could get.

Everything had been planned out very carefully. The Spaniards took most of the farming land for themselves, but they left the Indians just enough to live on. They made the Indians work for them on their big farms and ranches. They even tried to make the Indians give up the religion they had always practised in their kivas.

For a while the Indians didn't know what to do about all this. Naturally, they didn't like having their lives run for them. At last, almost all the different Pueblos joined together and rebelled, just the way the white colonies joined and rebelled nearly a hundred years later against the English king. The Indians loved their independence and freedom, and in 1680 they fought what some people call the First American Revolution. They drove the Spanish invaders out, and kept them away for twelve years.

The Spaniards had treated the Indians almost as slaves. But they had brought many new foods to Indian country and had taught the Pueblos new ways of doing things. Peach orchards now grew around many villages. Indian men wove the wool from sheep into blankets. The women learned to bake bread in ovens shaped like beehives, and sometimes they had mutton or beef to cook. Also the Pueblo Indians learned how to train and care for horses.

The Spaniards thought they had been very clever in making rules about horses when they first came. They were afraid the Indians would become too independent if they got the almost magic power that riding could give them. So they ordered Indians not to ride.

Of course the rule didn't work out. The Pueblos secretly learned to ride—after they got over their first fears of the strange foreign animals.

When the Spaniards fled from the Indians in 1680, they left most of their horses behind. During the twelve years they were gone, the horses had many colts. Now an interesting thing happened. Although the Pueblo Indians knew how to train and ride horses, they didn't really need the animals. They had no plows and they didn't live by hunting. But they could trade the horses to hunting tribes to the north, teaching them at the same time all their riding skills.

The horse, which made no great difference in the lives of the Pueblo Indians, completely changed the lives of most of the tribes on the Great Plains.

CHAPTER 16

Horses Change Men

OLD GET-THERE was a horse, a mare. That hadn't been her name when a Spanish rancher rode her. But now that the Spaniards were gone, the Pueblo Indians called her that. She was slow and awkward, but she always managed to get there, and she didn't care who rode her.

Old Get-There looked around patiently whenever a strange rider grabbed her mane and made a clumsy leap onto her back. She was used to the nervous squeeze of bare, brown legs on her sides, and she never bucked when a frightened rider pulled too hard on the single rein that ran to a loop around her lower jaw. Get-There just walked slowly around the corral, paying no attention to friends of the rider who joked and shouted as he learned the marvelous tricks of horsemanship.

One day the audience was a group of Comanches who had come all the way from Colorado. They had heard about the Pueblos' horses, and they wanted to trade buffalo hides for some of the wonderful animals.

The Comanches had made a strange-looking procession as they walked into the pueblo. The men carried their weapons and personal belongings. The women had babies on cradle boards or great bundles of hides on their backs. And the dogs looked strangest of all. Each one was hitched to two poles tied together over its shoulders, and across the poles was lashed a bundle for it to drag.

The Comanches stayed many days at the pueblo. They stayed until all the men had taken riding lessons, and some of the women, too. Meanwhile they had made their loads lighter. They traded all their buffalo robes for Get-There and two other mares that had been broken for riding. The Pueblo Indians made them a present of a wild young stallion that had never been ridden at all.

Finally the visitors were ready to go back north to their hunting grounds. Their chief, One Horn, and two other hunters rode the mares. The dogs, with small burdens on their drag poles, barked at the horses. The young stallion, who was led by a rope, shied and kicked one of the dogs.

Comanches came all the way from

Right away he got his name. The hunters laughed and called him Fix-with-the-Foot.

Weeks later the Comanches reached the Great Plains east of the Rockies. There the hunters sighted a huge herd of buffalo. The three riders shot more animals than they ever had before. Life was going to be much easier.

A RED STONE PIPE BUYS A HORSE

One summer, when the Comanches had followed the buffalo far north into Wyoming, they came across a large encampment of Indians who lived in poor makeshift tepees. And there was not a horse in sight.

Colorado to buy the Pueblos' horses

Chief One Horn gave the sign of peace as he approached. The women, he noticed, were cooking in clay pots, just the way the Pueblo women had done. These people must be farmers, although he saw no cornfields.

By using sign language, One Horn found out that this was a village of Cheyennes, and their chief was called No Fool. A short time before, Sioux warriors had driven No Fool's people from their farms in Minnesota. Now their supply of corn was almost gone.

When No Fool saw what the Comanche hunters could do with horses, he wanted some for his own men to use. But what did he have to trade? Luckily he observed the great interest the visitors took in the beautifully carved red stone pipes that he and his men smoked around the ceremonial fire. Possibly he could trade pipes for horses. He tried, and it worked.

Now old Get-There had new masters. For all the rest of her life she allowed scores of Cheyenne Indians to learn riding on her back. Before she was too old to be of any use, she was part of a large band of horses the Cheyennes managed to get by trading, or by the much more highly approved method of stealing from other tribes.

TRICKING THE BUFFALO

Meantime, the Cheyennes hunted on foot. Using an ancient trick, they disguised themselves in wolfskins and crept up among the buffalo. A big herd never paid much attention to a few wolves. They knew their horns and hoofs were protection enough against sharp wolf fangs. So a hunter in a wolfskin could steal up close, then use his bow and arrow. Of course he ran the danger of being trampled, and he could not get many animals at once.

The Cheyennes might have suffered badly from hunger if they hadn't found buffalo trails occasionally at the places where the plains broke into high bluffs. Then everybody went to work building a trap. They heaped up rounded walls of earth, stones, and grass clumps in the shape of a letter V. The wide opening of the V was toward the buffalo trail. The sides led to the cliff top.

Now they must wait until the herd approached along the trail. As they waited, the buffalo caller got ready for his job. He had become one of the most important men in the tribe. He knew all about the great humpbacked animals—their movements and their ways of living. At the right time he had to coax the herd into the trap.

At last the scouts reported that a herd was close. All but the younger children brought skins and robes from the tepees, hurried to the walls of the trap, and hid.

Suddenly a few big animals came in sight. The buffalo caller went out to meet them. His shoulders were covered with the hide of a buffalo calf. He moved quickly, swaying his body from side to side, with the buffalo's zigzag motion. Every once in a while he stopped and lowered his shoulders so that the hanging calf's head appeared to be grazing. Then he began to run around in circles to catch the eye of the leaders of the herd.

As soon as the caller had the huge beasts' attention, he gave the cry of a wounded calf and began to run toward the wide opening in the V-shaped trap. The bulls gave chase. The herd behind them took fright and followed.

The buffalo caller let the lead bulls come dangerously close to be sure they would go where he wanted them to. Then he raced at full speed, and the herd thundered after him. As soon as the animals entered the trap, the

Cheyennes jumped from their hiding places, yelling and shouting and waving their robes. The caller leaped aside and the panic-stricken herd thundered over the cliff. Any buffalo that did not die in the fall were killed with arrows or spears or by the blows of stone hammers.

As soon as the Cheyennes had horses enough, the old task of trap building disappeared. Now the men could hunt in easier ways, and they usually got all the meat they needed. They moved around so much that the clay pots of their farming days were a nuisance, and the women quit making them. They could store everything they needed in buffalo skins. They learned how to make jerked meat, cutting the fresh meat into thin slices and drying it in the sun, so that it would keep a long time. They pounded some of the dried meat to powder and mixed it with dried berries. This was pemmican, a wonderfully nourishing food that hunters could carry in buffalo-skin pouches on long trips.

When the Cheyennes had been farmers, they lived in houses made of poles and piled-up sod or mud. Now they had tepees big enough for whole families, because they had plenty of skins—and skill. The huge tepees were heavy, but that didn't matter. The horses were trained to pull burdens on big drag poles, called travois.

After a while nobody in the tribe walked. The Cheyennes felt as if they had been given wings.

Young men on a buffalo hunt rode light. They stripped off all their clothes except moccasins and breechcloths. They even left their quivers behind. In one hand they held the horse's single rein. In the other they carried their short, powerful bows and half a dozen arrows.

Riding bareback, they galloped in on the herd from

all sides and bunched it together so it wouldn't stampede. This roundup had to be very carefully organized. Each man had to obey rules and cooperate, or else he might make the whole tribe lose a chance to get the food it needed. Now horses and men showed their skill and initiative. Each hunter spotted the one buffalo in the milling herd that he wanted to shoot first. He edged up close, then dropped the rein across the horse's neck, and the horse took over. Keeping away from the beast's horns, the horse separated that particular buffalo from all the rest. He had been trained to dodge and nudge and worry the animal, which was three times as heavy as an Indian pony, and get it out onto the open plain. There the horse ran in pursuit close to the buffalo's right side. The rider leaned far forward over his pony's left shoulder, drew his bow with all his might, and let the arrow fly.

Sometimes a hunter shot with such power that the arrow went in up to the feather. Occasionally a shot went clear through the buffalo's thick body and came out the other side. Time and again, until all his arrows had been used, the hunter returned to the herd, and his horse cut out more animals to be shot. When the men had all they needed, they let the remainder of the herd escape.

FACTORY ON THE PLAINS

Meantime the women were busy, too. They packed up the tepees and all their belongings, put them on travois, and followed the men to the hunting ground. Now there was a great bustle but no confusion. Special policemen directed traffic. Tepees went up again in a circle, each in its own place, according to a regular plan. Skinning and cutting knives came out of the packs.

Cheyennes learned to shoot buffalo on horseback

And for days everyone worked from dawn to dark.

Here was a great factory on the open plain. Some women scraped the buffalo skins and stretched them out to dry. Some sliced the meat thin and hung it in the sun. Some carefully cut out the sinews that joined the muscles to the bones and saved them for bowstrings and thread and cord. Others made kettles from rawhide and filled them with buffalo hoofs and water. Then they boiled the water by dropping in hot stones. At last they had a sticky mass of glue that helped to make bows and arrows strong.

There was almost no part of a buffalo that went to waste. When the women finished their work, the Cheyennes had almost everything they needed to live on, and everything was shared equally among all. Here are some of the things a buffalo gave them:

Horns for headdresses and tools and spoons
Skins for winter robes and tepee covers, for moccasins and bags
Rawhide for saddles and thongs
Stomachs for bags
Bone marrow to eat
Teeth for ornaments
Shoulder blades for digging tools
Brains to be mashed and smeared onto hides as a softener
Droppings for fuel
Leftovers for the dogs to eat

This was a great deal of wealth—all just for shooting an arrow from horseback—and there were 30,000,000 buffalo on the Great Plains. No wonder the Cheyennes and many other tribes were content to follow the herds and forget that they ever had been quiet farmers hoeing corn! Horses had made a great change in the lives of men.

CHAPTER 17

Growing Up on the Plains

WHEN LOOK-AROUND was a very small boy he started to school. His classroom was the great open prairie or a grove of trees or the back of a horse, and his teacher was his uncle Rain-Walker. At first Look-Around had lessons in hunting and riding and nature study. Then he learned about the habits of buffalo—and the habits of men. Buffalo were just as important to other Indians of the Great Plains as they were to Look-Around's own people, the Cheyennes. It often happened that two different tribes wanted to hunt the same herd. And then there was a fight.

One fight led to another. The tribe that lost a battle retreated in anger and often sought revenge. People fought over horses, too. Those who had the best ones had the best chance of eating well. So the tribes raided each other's bands of horses. And this, of course, started more wars. Plains Indians did not believe it was wrong to steal horses, or anything else, from enemies. But they had strict rules against stealing from people in their own tribe. Look-Around learned never to cheat or lie to a Cheyenne.

Rain-Walker taught Look-Around to recognize his enemies simply by the prints their moccasins left in the earth. There were the Sioux to the north, mountaineering Utes to the west, Kiowas and Comanches to the south.

In all of Colorado and Wyoming only the Arapahoes were friendly to the Cheyennes.

HUNTERS HAD TO FIGHT

With enemies all around, the Cheyennes had to become warriors as well as hunters. They were a tall, proud, handsome people, and they trained themselves to be daring in battle—as daring even as the Sioux.

Before Look-Around learned about fighting, he and all the other boys of the plains became expert riders. Then they had make-believe battles on horseback. Rain-Walker taught Look-Around how to use his horse as a shield against enemy arrows and lances. First he took a rope and braided both ends into his horse's mane, making a loop under the neck. Now Look-Around could put his arm through the loop and slip clear over, leaving only one foot hooked across the horse's back. Except for the foot, he was completely protected from an enemy. Look-Around practised until he could ride this way at a full gallop.

When Look-Around left his tepee in the morning, Rain-Walker told him to study everything he saw all day long. Then at night Rain-Walker asked many questions, to find out how carefully he had watched and figured things out.

"What birds did you see today?" he asked. "What markings did they have? What were their habits? Did you notice any difference in the colors of the bark on opposite sides of a cottonwood tree?"

Rain-Walker taught Look-Around the safest approach to a grizzly bear in its den. You stole up from the rear, then threw something down in front of the opening.

That would make the bear come out to see what was happening. The bear would stop a moment before glancing behind him. Then, the instant he turned, you sent an arrow into his heart.

COURAGE AND SKILL

Look-Around had to practise enduring hardship, too. Sometimes Rain-Walker woke him at dawn and challenged him to go without eating all day. Look-Around wanted to be a great hunter and warrior, so he had to accept the challenge. To let everybody know they were fasting, he and his uncle blackened their faces with charcoal. Then all day long other boys did their best to tempt Look-Around with food.

Other mornings Rain-Walker waked him with a shrill war whoop in his ear. This trained Look-Around to jump up ready to fight and to yell out his own war whoop.

As Look-Around grew older he had to pass other tests. He learned how to tell direction, even on the flat, treeless prairie, by day or by night. He had to travel through strange enemy territory in the dark. And he had to take part in hard athletic games. Day after day he ran races on foot or on horseback. He competed in bow-and-arrow contests, which trained him to shoot fast and without even taking time to sight. Sometimes he shot arrows almost straight up into the sky, one right after the other, as fast as possible. The boy who had the most arrows in the air at one time won a prize.

Look-Around learned to swim, so that he could cross big rivers in the plains if he had to. And he wrestled. Sometimes all the boys wrestled at the same time. The winner was the one who never got thrown off his feet. These matches were rough-and-tumble and almost anything was fair. But the boys never showed pain. They were learning to stand all kinds of hardship with bravery. Look-Around's athletic training was harder and lasted longer than the training of boxers or football players today.

THE BIG BALL GAME

In summer, the men and boys played ball when all the different bands of Cheyennes gathered together for the annual meeting of the whole tribe. Hundreds played at once—sometimes even a thousand, divided into two teams on an immense field.

Men and boys played the game barefoot. They wore nothing but their leather breechcloths and a kind of ceremonial bustle made of stiff horsehair. They all looked as if they had tails like horses—and they ran as long and almost as fast as if they were.

A ball game sometimes lasted all day, with only a minute or two of rest each time a goal was scored. The players had to be in wonderful condition to keep on from morning till night, but they loved the game, and so did the fans who crowded around to watch. Afterward came feasting and dancing.

The tribal meeting was fun—and it was important, too. This was the time for electing the forty councilors or chiefs who advised the four great chiefs of the whole Cheyenne tribe. The chiefs were the leaders and judges, chosen for their wisdom and courage.

After the summer meeting, the different Cheyenne bands separated and took up their wandering again. But they needed to keep in touch with each other, and so they used smoke signals.

Look-Around and the other boys learned to build a signal fire and then cover it with a buffalo robe to collect smoke. When they pulled the robe off, they let a puff of smoke rise in the air. Three puffs going up at the same time from three fires meant "Danger!" There were many other signals, and by using them one band could send messages in relays for hundreds of miles in a few hours.

Rain-Walker taught Look-Around two other necessary things. The first was sign language. It was important because many different tribes roamed the Great Plains, each with its own spoken language. The Cheyennes could not understand a word that most of these tribes spoke. But when two tribes were on friendly terms, it was useful to exchange news about enemy war parties or good hunting grounds. So the Indians invented sign language. By making different motions with their hands, people of all the plains tribes could talk to each other.

Although the Plains Indians could not read or write, they had another way of keeping records and sending messages. They used a kind of picture language that explained what they wanted to say. Each picture told a story that anyone could understand.

ALMOST A MAN

Like almost all young Indian boys, Look-Around was eager to become a warrior and win honors in battle against an enemy tribe. He waited especially for the day when he could put on a large eagle-feather war bonnet. Indians thought that the eagle was the mightiest of all birds and brought great power to warriors. That is why they wore an eagle feather in their hair or in their bonnets for each honor that they had won.

When a warrior had many honors he could join a club of the bravest men in his tribe. The members were called "brave dogs," "old dogs," "crazy dogs," or something like that. Later on, when white men came, they called the Cheyenne warriors "dog soldiers," which meant that they respected the Indians very much for their bravery and skill.

As Look-Around listened to tales of battle and worked at the lessons his uncle taught, he was gradually learning how to live in the world around him. It was a hard world of struggle against nature and sometimes against other men. He knew he must be able to stand any pain if he was to be useful to his people. From the time he was a little boy, his uncle prepared him for a great test to prove his courage and endurance.

The test came at a joyous festival called the Sun Dance. Part of it seems strange and horrible to us, but the Indians thought it was a good way of training men to live in a land where only the strong could survive.

The festival began with secret ceremonies in the tepee at the center of the camp. The young men who were taking part for the first time fasted and listened to talks by medicine men. Outside the sacred tepee, men gathered poles and set them firmly in the ground in a circle.

Then they began to beat drums and dance. Everyone gave gifts to orphans and to widows who had no men to hunt for them. The beat of drums and the chanting of singers rose louder and louder. Suddenly all this stopped. The young men came from the ceremonial tepee. With a great war cry, the dancers rushed upon them and pretended to fight a battle in which the young men lost.

Now the young men lay motionless on the ground. They made no sound as medicine men pierced holes in the flesh of their backs or chests and thrust wooden sticks through the slits. Some had buffalo skulls attached by leather thongs to the cuts in their backs. Others, who had already proved they were brave warriors, were tied up off the ground on the sacred poles. They hung there by thongs attached to the sticks that pierced the flesh of their breasts.

As a signal was given, the dance began. Throughout the long hot day, except for a few rest periods, the young men danced with the buffalo skulls hanging from the skin of their backs. Finally the moment came for escape from their bonds. People helped them pull against the thongs, trying to jerk so that their flesh would tear and release them. Those who fainted were carried away. They were considered weaklings. Those who finished the dance with honor would be able to fight well for their people.

Look-Around had watched the Sun Dance ever since he could remember. It frightened him at first, but he got used to the idea, and now he even looked forward to the honor of proving his own courage. But long before he was old enough to join in the Sun Dance, he had to go through other special ceremonies.

When he was about fourteen, he and the other boys his age had a very important experience. Each one left the camp alone and went out in search of his special guardian spirit, who would help him in hunting and fighting and perhaps make him a leader of his band.

To find his guardian spirit, Look-Around had to do

everything exactly according to rule. If he didn't, he would anger the Great Spirit, leader of all other spirits.

First Look-Around had to purify himself in mind and in body. For this he took a sweat bath in a little hut, where he crouched down and made steam by sprinkling water on hot stones. Then he dashed out naked to a nearby stream and plunged into the cold water.

Now he was ready to seek the vision. Next morning at daybreak he set out with the medicine man for a distant hill. There the old man left him alone to fast and pray to the Great Spirit.

At the beginning of every prayer, he took his red stone pipe and pointed it solemnly in the four directions. Day after day, and night after night, he lay on the bare ground without a drop of water to drink or a bit of food to eat.

Finally, he saw his vision in a dream. Rejoicing, Look-Around returned to camp with a song of victory on his lips. He had dreamed that he saw and talked with a black-tailed deer. But, since he didn't know the meaning of his vision, he went to the medicine man of the Black-tailed Deer Club. The medicine man explained that, like the deer, Look-Around would always be able to scent any danger.

Now Look-Around had to perform a dance, dressed as a deer. And ever afterward he was supposed to carry a charm made of sage. This was the deer's food, and it would give him protection.

All these things—the games, the fasts, the learning about horses and bows and arrows, the tortures and visions and charms—were part of growing up to be a hunter and a warrior on the plains.

CHAPTER 18

The Largest Tribe

THE HUNTERS OF THE PLAINS were not the only Indians whose lives were greatly changed by the horses that came first from the Spaniards, then from the Pueblos. The Navahos learned about horses, too, and they took up many other new ways that completely changed their lives.

The story of the Navahos starts around the time when the Cliff Dwellers moved away from the mesas. About then, the Navahos were coming into the Southwest. At first they were just a weak branch of the Apache tribe who had traveled all the way from Canada, where some of their relatives remain to this day.

The Navaho group was quick to learn farming and weaving from the Pueblos. They also borrowed ceremonies and ways of making beautiful paintings out of colored sands and pollens. After the Spaniards came with their horses, the Navahos turned into expert horsemen. They learned how to make things from silver and other metals, and they took up herding the sheep and goats that the white men brought along.

All this knowledge made the Navahos grow stronger. For a while they used their strength to raid other tribes in order to become still stronger. But they also kept improving the new arts they had learned. Sheep herding became more and more the main work of the tribe. From the sheep's wool came the lovely blankets that they still weave. And Navahos still do handsome silver work and make beautiful drawings and sing beautiful poems. Instead of remaining a branch of the Apache tribe, the Navahos have become the largest and most important Indian tribe in the United States. They are vigorous, proud people, full of life and good jokes.

On the Navaho reservation in Arizona today, there is a trading post where people like to gather and swap yarns. One morning an old man told this story to some friends:

"Long ago," said the old man, "a white god came down on top of Navaho Mountain, bringing some of the white fire that lights up the stars. When he went back to the sky, he got a little absent-minded and left a few pieces of the white fire behind.

"Next day, some children playing on the mountain picked up the white fire and took it home. They could do this without getting burned, of course. Everybody knows that the white fire of the gods gives no heat.

"At first the Navahos were very glad to have the light from the white fire, but they soon found that it had one bad habit. Every little piece of it kept on growing and growing, and there was no way to put it out. It filled up the hogans [houses]. Then it spread outside. Finally it covered the whole valley where the children lived.

"The medicine men had to ask the god for help. They talked and argued with him, and at last he agreed to make a bargain. He would take all the white fire back if the people in the valley would let him dump all the white ashes from the white fire in the stars down on their valley during the winter time.

"That's why it still snows in the valley every year."

All the Navahos in the trading post listened very soberly to this story, and thought about it for a while. Then a young know-it-all asked, "If that's true, why does it snow everywhere else too?"

The old man snorted. "My young friend, this valley is where I live. Let people who live some place else make up their own stories."

Navahos love the country where they live. They say many poetic things about it—and they also love to joke. They are full of life—so full of life that their tribe is growing faster than any other group of people in the United States. In fact, the Navahos have grown so much that they are actually a whole distinct nation right inside our country. The land where they live is larger than Massachusetts, Connecticut, and New Hampshire combined. That is a lot of space, but the Navahos feel crowded there, and they really are. Each year they spread out farther around the edges of their reservation, which is in Arizona and the near-by parts of New Mexico and Utah.

The Navahos, who call themselves Dineh, meaning The People, need lots of space. A great many of them are shepherds, and their flocks must have great areas to graze in. Others are ranchers and farmers. They need space too. There isn't enough grass in the whole reservation to feed all the sheep and goats and cattle that the Navahos must raise in order to make a living. So they are poor, very poor. On an average, each Navaho earns less than a hundred dollars a year. The men can't get food by hunting as they used to. The game is gone because the grass is gone.

In spite of the great troubles the Navahos have today, they still love their land. They have lived there for the last five hundred years or more. It is a varied and wonderfully beautiful land. Mesas made of bright colored rocks jut up from flat valleys covered with soft gray-green sagebrush. Deep canyons gash the high plateaus and steep gullies wind snakelike through the flat bottomlands. Travel anywhere in a straight line is impossible. Here is a place where the long way around is always the shortest. Old volcanoes thrust up out of the desert, and great pine-covered mountain ranges cut across the country. Clumps of juniper and piñon pine add their dark dusty-green to the landscape, and over it all is the most brilliant of blue, blue skies.

The dry, sparkling air of Navaholand is ideal for healthy living. In fact, white people go to many health resorts near by. But the Navahos, in the midst of their wonderful climate, have much more tuberculosis than other Americans. They are just too poor to get enough of the right food and medicines. There are government hospitals now, of course, and hospitals run by Christian churches, but not nearly enough of them. So the old time medicine man—the Navahos call him the Singer—does a thriving business.

Modern doctors look at what the Singers do, and they naturally disapprove. But people who love art and poetry see a great deal of beauty in the Navaho curing ceremonies. Here is what happens:

When a Navaho is sick, he calls in a Singer and gives him horses or sheep to conduct a ceremony. The Singer has spent a great deal of time learning what to do, so he must be paid well. Then the man's family and all his

A young Navaho shepherd watching his flock

dozens of relatives and even many friends gather at his hogan.

The Singer comes and spreads a white buckskin on the hogan floor. He covers it with pure-white sand. Then, while he and his helpers sing the proper songs, he carefully sprinkles colored earths and yellow pollen on the sand to make a bright, sacred picture. His fingers are so skillful that the picture is really a beautiful painting on the sand. The Singer knows many different songs and dances and prayers, for different kinds of sickness.

The prayers may be to Changing Woman, the most important Navaho god. She is the one who does good things and tries to help people out. Her husband, the Sun, isn't always so helpful—and there must be prayers asking him to do good instead of evil. The Singer may also pray to the children of Changing Woman and the Sun—the Hero Twins. They are called Monster Slayer and Child of Water, and they often do very mean things. Navahos try to stay on the good side of these Hero Twins.

A ceremony to win the help of the gods may go on all night, or even four or five days. But the sick man knows that all the people who love him are trying to make up to the gods for something wrong he must have done. Navahos believe that no one gets sick unless he has done something wrong. Often it does help a sick person to know that people love him and are trying to help.

Ceremonies are held for many other things besides sickness. Navahos have religious beliefs and customs about everything they do.

Parents arrange many of the marriages, for instance, and the bride's parents are always supposed to receive a gift or payment from the bridegroom. Navaho men who can afford it sometimes have more than one wife. That is perfectly all right, according to their religion. Their marriage customs are serious, but Navahos love to tell jokes about them, too. Here is a favorite story:

A man had several daughters, and he managed to get them all married but one. She was the ugliest creature alive. She was nearly bald. She had no teeth. Her face would scare a varmint, and she was so fat that three people could hide behind her.

But the man kept trying to find her a husband, although she was well over forty years old.

One day he met a Navaho who came from way off in the Painted Desert. The father thought that perhaps he could trick this man into marrying his daughter, and so he started talking to him.

"My daughter is the most beautiful creature in Navaholand," he boasted. "I am sure that only you can make her happy."

The father went on like that and got carried away with his own words. Finally he began talking about her "beautiful black hair that hung to the ground, and her teeth that were so white that they shone like the stars at night."

The man from the Painted Desert looked quietly at the boastful father. Then he said, "Well, I'll tell you what. I've heard of your beautiful daughter, and it makes me sad that I can't buy her from you so that I can marry her. But I have already promised to buy three other females—a wild cat, a hoot owl, and a donkey. I will give you the donkey, and you can keep your daughter."

After a man is married, he must keep one very strict religious rule: He and his mother-in-law are never supposed to look at each other as long as they live. You can imagine how difficult this is when you realize that a Navaho man is always supposed to move in with his wife's family. He and his mother-in-law may live in hogans very close together, but for all the years of their lives, they have to keep out of each other's sight. Here is a Navaho joke about that problem:

One man met another outside a trading post. Just for the fun of it, he told him that his mother-in-law was inside. The newcomer went off out of sight to wait for her to leave. After waiting patiently for an hour he began to suspect a joke was being played on him. No one had brought him word that his mother-in-law was gone. So he asked a friend who was walking by to go inside the trading post and see if the coast was clear. This man came back after a while and shook his head sadly.

"My friend," he said, "I really don't know if your mother-in-law is in there or not. You have never told me just who all your wives are!"

Actually as a rule a man has only one wife. The couple live in a hogan, way out in the desert somewhere, with only one or two or three other hogans near by. Most Navahos don't live in villages. They have to be out on the land where their cattle, sheep and goats can graze.

So the hogans are usually far from any road, but as near as possible to water and wood. Sometimes that means living ten or fifteen miles away from a spring or a grove of trees. There may not be even one tree for shade.

Each hogan has only one room, and it is roughly round and dome-shaped, made of logs covered with mud. There is only one door, and a smoke hole in the roof. The thick windowless walls keep out much of the heat in summer and make the room warm in winter. When the weather is bad, women cook over an open fire, or a stove if they have one, in the center of the room, right under the smoke hole. On fine days they cook outdoors, and the family eats under a "shade"—a roof of brush held up by posts to keep the sun off. There a sheepskin with the wool side down is spread for a tablecloth, and each member of the family dips into one big dish with his own spoon. The main food is mutton or goat meat from the family's own animals and bread made of white flour that comes from the trading post.

COWBOY CLOTHES

Usually Navaho boys and girls and old folks herd the sheep and goats. Children even start having flocks of their own when they are very young. A large flock is one of the most important things in Navaho life. The men take care of their horses and cattle and do all the things that have to be done around any small sheep or cattle ranch. In addition to these chores, they make their own saddles.

As they go about their work, the men and boys dress much like all cowboys and ranch hands in the Southwest—in big wide-brimmed hats and blue denim pants. But instead of ordinary work shirts, they often wear bright-colored ones with gay scarves. And in place of undershorts, they wear breechcloths just like the ones their ancestors wore ages ago. The old moccasins are not forgotten, either. Although most Navaho men have shoes or cowboy boots, they are likely to keep moccasins tucked away between the logs of their hogans and to bring them out for special ceremonies or dances.

Some Navaho men keep their hair in long braids and

others have short haircuts the way white men do. But almost all the women stick to one style they learned long ago from the Pueblos. They comb their hair straight back and make it into a big roll at the back of the neck.

The Navaho women have borrowed their dress styles too, but not from the Pueblos. They got the idea of very long, full skirts from Spanish women and from the wives of officers in the United States Army almost a hundred years ago. Navaho skirts are made of bright calico. The blouses are calico, too, or velveteen—and always in bright colors. For coats or shawls the women always carry blankets with them to wear in public, except in the hottest weather. The men carry blankets only when it is cold.

You might expect these blankets to be the beautiful Navaho kind that are so famous—but they usually aren't. They are ordinary machine-made blankets bought from a trader. Almost all the handmade blankets go to the trading post, for sale to white people. Women weave them, using the wool they themselves have sheared from their own sheep and twisted into yarn by hand. In good weather they sit outdoors under a "shade" and work their intricate designs. Sometimes the colors they use are made from plants they gather. Or the dye may come from the trader.

Take a good look at a Navaho blanket the next time you see one. You will find what looks like a mistake in it somewhere. Every real Navaho rug has a "mistake," and this is the reason: The weaver leaves one place that is not finished and perfect, so that his spirit will not be trapped inside the rug. There must always be a way for the weaver's spirit to get out.

Navahos think it is unlucky to make a perfect blanket, just as some people you know think it is unlucky to walk under a ladder, or to break a mirror. Navahos have lots of beliefs like this. They say it is unlucky to step over anyone who is asleep. No matter how crowded a hogan is with people sleeping on the floor, no one ever steps across anyone else.

Navahos never kill a snake or a coyote or certain kinds of birds. You may think this is silly, but it happens that these particular customs have turned out to be useful. Snakes and coyotes kill prairie dogs, and prairie dogs ruin crops and grazing land. Grasshoppers eat up crops too, but birds eat grasshoppers.

Navahos have other beliefs that often get white people all mixed up. For example, each Navaho has a secret name. It is one of his most important possessions, and he believes that it gets worn out if it is used. So he almost never uses it. Neither does anyone else. It is even impolite to call a person by his nickname when he is around. Most Navahos have one nickname—sometimes two. His family uses one in speaking about him, and outsiders use the other.

Besides these names, Navahos often acquire still others. They never have any family names of their own, but traders and teachers and employers are so used to the white man's custom that they just *give* family names to Navahos. A Spanish-speaking farmer may call a Navaho who works for him José Martinez. The English-speaking trader who sells him food may call him John Left Hand. The teacher may think that Left Hand is a funny sounding last name when she enrolls his child in school, so she may decide a better one is John Marshall. And if this same Navaho is drafted into the army, he may get still another. It may be John Wagon Spoke—the nickname the army recruiting sergeant hears from other Navahos.

To the Navaho all this fuss about names seems very funny. He knows exactly who he is and what his real name is—and he's not telling!

JEWELRY IN THE DESERT

Just as women do the weaving, men often specialize in making silver jewelry. Navahos learned this art long ago from the Spaniards, and they still hammer out beautiful designs, working with very little equipment. Often the only anvil they have is a short chunk of railroad rail fastened to a log.

The jewelry and the blankets help bring money to the people on the reservation. So does work on railroads and highways. But most Navahos can work only at common labor. Although they have great skills of their own, they have never until recently had much of a chance to learn how to do skilled work in factories or shops. Also it is hard for Navahos to live away from home. White people often do not treat them as equals. They cannot eat in restaurants or sleep in hotels near the reservation. This kind of thing naturally makes them angry, and they often return home to be with their own people, who lead a democratic life.

Many young Navahos go to government schools and mission schools on the reservation. There they learn to be carpenters and mechanics and nurses and office workers. For a long time children learned very little at school, because their teachers couldn't speak Navaho and there were no books for them to study in their own language. Now some teachers are Navahos themselves. Others have learned the language. A Navaho alphabet has been worked out, so that children can have their own special kind of books. This helps them a great deal in learning to read and write the English language. Still, there are not nearly enough schools. The number of children who speak only Navaho is growing faster than the number who also learn English. And nearly half the children on the reservation never have a chance to go to school.

TRIBAL COUNCIL

The tribal council and the headmen or chiefs among the Navahos are working hard to solve this problem, and many others. A headman is a man whom everyone in his neighborhood recognizes as the best leader. Navahos don't vote him in or out of office. They just talk things over until everyone agrees on a headman.

Members of the tribal council are chosen at regular elections. The council runs the affairs of the nation with the help of the Navaho Service, which is part of the Indian Service of the United States Government. This council is new. Navahos never had one chief, or one governing council, until 1923.

Now the Navahos are looking toward the future, and their leaders are working on plans to bring more of the good things of life to their people. They know that their land can't produce a living for more than half of them.

There are already too many animals in Navaholand. They eat the grass faster than it can grow. As the grass disappears, rains wash away the topsoil, leaving nothing for grass to grow on at all. The whole country is becoming a desert.

Some new way of living has to be found. Perhaps before too long Navahos will find a way to have factories and businesses that will give work to the great number of them who can't live off the land in the old way.

The leaders know that modern industry and science, which the white men brought, have made America a much richer and better place to live in than it was in the days when Indians knew nothing of these things. Navahos, and all Indians, may resent the way modern inventions and efficiency have often been used against them. But they are learning that they must have these things work for them in the future.

Perhaps before too long Navahos will find a way to keep more of the wealth that is now taken from underneath the dry Navaho soil. There is oil there, and rare helium gas, and vanadium, which is needed for atomic energy. And there are places where great dams could be built, saving water for irrigation and electric power.

There is a way for the Navahos, and they love life so much that they will surely find it. They will take their place as equals in every way with all other Americans in using and enjoying the best that modern life has to offer. But they will always be Navaho Americans—and proud of it.

CHAPTER 19

Great Cities in the Jungle

At sunrise in the city of Chichén-Itzá, the festival of the harvest was about to begin. For many days, thousands of Maya Indians from all over Yucatán had walked on beautiful paved roads through the jungles. Now they filled the city, where a white temple stood on a high pyramid at one side of an immense square.

This festival was a time of happiness and joy. The people laughed as they wandered in the covered market place that ran around three sides of the square, its roof supported by a thousand round stone columns, each thicker than a man. With cocoa seeds for money, they could buy everything from hot tamales to necklaces of jade or gold or curious sea shells. Some stalls offered the brilliant feathers of tropical birds for sale. Others had pottery or fine cotton cloth or tomatoes or wild-boar meat or that special delicacy, the tail of the iguana lizard. Meat markets sold small hairless dogs as well as wild ducks and turkeys and venison. Some stalls had honey that farmers had brought in from their hives of stingless bees. There were avocado pears and papaya and breadfruit.

But buying things was for later. The pilgrims had come for the harvest ceremony, where they would give thanks to the gods of rain and new-growing things.

After the ceremony had begun, two companies of warriors marched in and lined up near a terrace in the square. Their feathered helmets were shaped like birds or animals. In battle they wore heavy padded cotton armor, three inches thick, but today they had on decorated cotton skirts and high sandals.

Now wooden drums and gourd trumpets announced that the ruler of the city was coming. Eight men carried him on a magnificent chair that was enclosed so that no one could see him. When he stepped out, all the thousands of people in the square lowered their eyes. They knew they were not supposed to look at the face of their sacred leader. But as he walked to his throne up the terrace steps under a tasseled shade carried by a guard, many of them did catch a glimpse of his royal costume.

They saw his jeweled sandals walking on the fine tapestry that covered the stone stairway. They saw his pure-gold helmet with jewels sparkling in it and quetzal-bird feathers rising above. They saw his cape made from the feathers of a thousand bright-colored birds, his jade and gold jewelry, his skirt interwoven with threads of gold, his knee protectors of the finest down of birds.

The ruler reached his shining throne and sat down between his wife and his oldest son. Next the high priest came up the stairs, and after him marched slaves carrying the best fruits and vegetables of the first harvest.

At last the high priest blew incense all around and signaled for the waiting thousands to lie flat on the ground in prayer. Then he placed the fruits and vegetables on the altars of the gods and gave them thanks. With this, the

A Mayan high priest at the harvest ceremony

ceremony was over. The happy people rose and set about celebrating.

BASKETBALL GAME

Many went to the great basketball court opposite the market of a thousand columns. Nobles filled the reserved seats, showing off their jewels, their richly embroidered capes, and their fancy skin-covered wooden helmets. Among them sat priests in long flowing robes. The boys in the crowd had their faces painted black to show they were not married. The faces of the married men were all painted red. Farmers wearing only cotton capes and breechcloths crowded onto the stone seats behind the nobles and priests.

The ball field below was surrounded by a high stone wall, and on two opposite sides stone rings were set eighteen feet above the ground. They were like basketball rings, except they were higher in the air, and they hung upright like an automobile tire instead of parallel with the ground, like the rim of our basketball basket.

First a priest held a ceremony. Then fourteen players —seven for each team—ran into the court, and the priest threw down a big eight-pound solid-rubber ball.

The ball bounced high. A player hit it with his leather-padded hip as it came down. Hands were not allowed. Only elbows, wrists, shoulders, head, or hips could touch the ball, and each player tried to bounce it through one of the stone rings to score a point for his side.

Few points were ever made in a game, but the struggle between players was intense. When one team made the winning goal, pandemonium broke loose in the audience. Nobles and commoners and priests all made a good-natured dash to get away, regardless of which team they supported. The reason was simple. By ancient custom the player who made the winning goal had the right to seize any jewels or clothes he could get from the audience.

After the game came feasting and singing and dancing that lasted all night. Now the pilgrims could go home, feeling sure they had done everything possible to please the gods who made their corn grow.

JUNGLE FIELDS

The Mayas had other foods, of course, but corn was the most important. It grew from the jungle soil in almost magic abundance, and it had made possible all the other vast riches of their empire.

A farmer simply chopped down and burned off jungle trees and brush, made holes in the earth with his digging stick, and dropped seeds in. Sun and rain and the nourishing earth did the rest. Without bothering to irrigate or even to weed his fields, he grew for a few seasons much more corn than he could possibly use.

In the beginning, when corn was a brand-new discovery, the Indians of Central America had been no better off than all the others who struggled to get enough food. But with corn so easy to raise, families and tribes grew larger. People from other places heard about the jungle land that grew corn easily and they moved in. Before long, hundreds of thousands were enjoying the life they found in this warm country—a life that was much, much easier than any they had ever led before.

There was food enough so that people had a great deal of spare time. Some of them began to use that time well. They figured out something that every farmer wants to know—the answer to the question, "When is the best time to plant crops?"

FARMING BY THE STARS

You'd say the best time is naturally spring, after the cold winter is over, when the days are getting longer. But in places like Yucatán there is much less difference between winter and summer than where you live. People don't notice much change in temperature or in the length of days. They do know that there is a rainy season and a dry season. Corn has to be planted in Yucatán before the rainy season begins, so that it develops good strong shoots. But, unless you have a calendar, you have no sure way of knowing when the rains will begin. So some of the Indians began to figure out a calendar. But first, they had to know exactly how many days there were between the beginning of one spring and the beginning of the next. Watching the sun gave them the clue.

They found that the sun rose at different places on the horizon at different times of the year. From watching the sun in the sky, they got to watching the stars too. They found that the stars also moved in regular paths. And, as they observed both the sun and the stars, they had to develop more and more complicated ways of counting.

Like most peoples, the Mayas already had a simple way of counting. Perhaps they made marks with cornmeal on the walls of their homes, as other Indians did. Or perhaps they kept count by means of knots tied in strings. These simple methods of figuring are all right up to a point, but they aren't good enough for the long-drawn-out work of keeping track of sun and star movements for years and years. The Mayas needed permanent records. So they invented a way of writing down numbers and arithmetic problems.

After a long, long time, the men who specialized in sky-watching made a calendar out of the figures they had written down. A whole new knowledge had been added to the simple business of finding out when to plant crops.

Like many other peoples, the Mayas also believed there were lucky and unlucky days. Now, following the calendar, the astronomers told the farmers which days were which. They set the dates for performing the magical ceremonies that were supposed to bring the rain and make the crops grow. The astronomers actually became the bosses of the ceremonies. This gave them great power.

Gradually, the astronomers made the ceremonies more and more elaborate. They mixed old superstitions in with their way of measuring time. The calendar showed when temples should be built, what days were good for marriages and a lot of other things. So the common people grew more and more dependent on the learned astronomers. The sky-watchers became rulers over the whole lives of the people. The calendar, which started out by setting dates for the ceremonies that farmers believed would bring the rain, ended by controlling everything the Mayas did.

The farmers, working all together on the land they held in common, grew plenty of corn. So there was food enough for the astronomers, who spent all their time studying the stars. There was even enough food so that some men could give up farming and become weavers, jewelers, goldsmiths, or carvers of wood and stone. With abundance came time to make life more beautiful.

SCIENCE—AND SCIENCE FICTION

The learned men saw the power they held because of their knowledge, and they kept it to themselves. Gradually they added a lot of stories and superstitions to their true science of stars and numbers. They said they could prophesy all kinds of events by their calendar.

The astronomers passed on their science and their science fiction only to their sons. Little by little a class of nobles grew up. They became rulers and priests who lived in stone palaces in great cities. Far removed from them in every way were the common people, who still lived in mud-covered huts as simply as their ancient ancestors had.

The nobles used their knowledge of arithmetic to plan great buildings. They measured out size and shape precisely and directed the exact cutting of the stones. The commoners learned how to chisel perfectly formed blocks, although they had no iron tools.

The arithmetic the nobles used was made up of dots and dashes. One dot stood for the number 1; two dots for 2, and so on up through 4. A dash was 5, four dots and a dash made 9. Besides these numerals, they had a way of giving the name for each number with a kind of picture called a glyph.

The nobles made up more and more stories and rules about spirits and gods. And always they claimed they could prove their stories by the writing they learned how to put down in books. Instead of making words out of separate letters as we do, they made a separate picture for each word. There were so many different glyphs that it took a great deal of schooling before a boy was really good at reading and writing.

MAYA INVENTIONS

The Maya Indians began their farming and building and inventing many hundreds of years before Columbus discovered the New World. They had no knowledge of what other people had learned in other lands. They started from almost nothing and created their own civilization. Living mainly on their wonderful corn crops, they did these things by themselves:

They invented writing.

They invented their own numbers and arithmetic.

They invented a calendar. Only modern science, with its wonderful instruments, has figured out a more accurate way of measuring the year.

They made great buildings out of stones that were cut and shaped to exact size.

They built huge cities, some with room for more than 200,000 people.

They made long paved roads between cities.

They discovered how to make cement, and used it in their buildings, streets, roads, and the sewer systems under the cities.

They built pyramids, some of which were bigger than those in Egypt.

They carved beautiful sculptures, and made beautiful pottery and clothes and ornaments.

The Mayas did all these things, and many more, although they had no tools made of iron, no large animals like horses, and no wheels to help them with the work.

The Mayas grew to be the most civilized people in all of North and South America. They were peaceful and did not try to conquer other tribes. Each city had soldiers only to fight off enemy attacks.

But trouble began when the jealous rulers of different cities began to quarrel among themselves. Then wars between groups of Mayas broke out. At the same time, enemies came against them from outside.

Most important of all, the rich Maya soil wore out. The Mayas, who had learned so much about the stars, had never learned how to take care of the soil in which their corn grew. They did not know how to irrigate, cultivate, fertilize or keep soil from washing away.

The great day of Maya civilization was ended. But the things the Mayas invented were borrowed by other Indians. Some of their ideas spread as far as the cliff dwellings in Mesa Verde. Indians far off in the Mississippi Valley built pyramids. Nowadays we give the name Mound Builders to these people, who dotted our country with earthen pyramids. And closer to the Mayas, the warlike Aztecs followed them as the great Indian nation in Mexico.

Mound Builders hunted as well as farmed

CHAPTER 20

An Empire of Power and Fear

HERE IS A PROPHECY Aztec medicine men made long, long ago, when the tribe was wandering in North America:

"Someday we shall see an eagle with a snake in its beak, standing on a rock in a patch of cactus. That is a sign. There we must build our home."

The tribe made its way down into Mexico, hunting and fighting, hunting and fighting again. They were warriors, and indeed they had to be, for their journey took them through the lands of many different tribes.

At last one day they pushed forward into a great, pleasant valley in Mexico. All around were high mountains. In the distance a volcano sent up plumes of smoke, and at the center of the valley near a lake they found the sign they had been seeking for so many years—an eagle with a snake in its beak, standing on a rock in a patch of cactus!

Now their journey was ended—but not their troubles.

Other powerful tribes already lived all around the lake. There was no room for newcomers. Unless the strangers would settle on an island out in the middle of the lake, they would have to move along.

The Aztecs were a determined people. If they had to live on the island—well, they would. There was little to hunt out there except ducks, and no space to grow food as the farming tribes did along the shore. But the Aztecs had made up their minds they would get along, and they did. They studied their neighbors, whom they called Toltecs, meaning "Skilled Workers." Then they used what they learned.

Since they had no land for gardens, the Aztecs made land. First they gathered reeds that grew in the lake. When the long reed stems were tied into thick bundles lashed together, they floated lightly on the water. The Aztecs built many large rafts of reeds and piled rich mud from the lake bed on top. Now they could grow wonderful floating gardens, even trees, on their rafts. Before long the Aztecs had flowers and vegetables to trade in the markets of the Toltec cities.

BRIDGE BUILDERS

Gradually the Aztecs made friends with the Toltecs, who were peaceful people, much like the Mayas. Before long the Aztecs became the most powerful tribe around the lake. Keeping their knowledge about warfare, they learned all they could about building and other useful crafts. They needed this new knowledge to help carry out plans they were working on.

For one thing, it took a long time to paddle a dugout canoe from their island city to the mainland. That was all right for a farmer going to market. But suppose the chief wanted to send large numbers of soldiers across in a hurry. Dugouts were no good for that. And so the Aztecs undertook the enormous labor of building roads like bridges over the lake! Soon these causeways led away from the island city in all four directions, each of them several miles long.

Years went by, and still the Aztecs kept on learning

Aztec warriors were bold and frightening

and adopting new ideas. Like the Toltecs and the Mayas, they built huge pyramids with temples on top. They took up carving and writing and calendar making, which came to them from the Mayas. The Aztecs were great borrowers. Only two hundred years after they reached the shore of their lake, there was very little in the island city to remind them of their wandering ancestors—except their warriors' skill. Even that had changed into something new. Instead of just fighting to survive, the Aztecs began to conquer other tribes and make them pay tribute.

Finally the Aztec Empire stretched clear across one part of Mexico from the Pacific Ocean to the Gulf of Mexico. Each tribe the Aztecs defeated paid tribute every year according to its own special kind of wealth—for example, 24,000 bundles of magnificent feathers of all colors, or a certain number of amber earrings, or emeralds, or 200 sacks of cocoa beans, which were used as money, or rubber that slaves carried up from the lowland jungles on their backs, or gold that slaves dug out of the high mountains.

No matter how little a conquered tribe had, they must send something to their rulers. Farmers sent honey. One town paid its tribute in building stone. The very poorest paid in snakes, scorpions, and even pots full of dried lice!

HUMAN SACRIFICE

Aztec warriors were bold and frightening in their war paint and padded armor and huge gaudy-feathered helmets. But they did not kill many people in battle. In fact, they tried not to. They wanted to capture, not to kill. First of all, they wanted slaves to work on the vast buildings that were always going up. But they had another reason for taking captives, too, and it is one that we find very hard to understand. Aztecs believed that they had to offer human beings as sacrifices to their gods. Other tribes only sacrificed valuable things such as food or animals. They believed that they should give back something to the earth from which they had taken food away. This idea was part of their religion. The Aztecs wanted to be as religious as possible, so they gave back to the earth the most valuable thing of all—human blood. They killed thousands of human beings in their temples.

In spite of this cruel and bloody custom, the Aztecs were almost always loyal and kindly to each other. They never locked their doors, because they could feel sure nothing would be stolen while they were away from home. But their warlike habit of violence did show itself in one way that makes them different from almost all other Indians. They sometimes used whips of painful stinging nettles to punish children who lied or broke rules. Other Indians, even the most warlike, seldom even spanked children. If boys or girls misbehaved, grownups only showed disapproval, and children felt this was just as real a punishment as any other.

RULES, RULES, RULES

Aztec children were brought up according to strict rules. A three-year-old was allowed only half a cake of cornbread for each meal. A four- or five-year-old got a whole cake. The ration went up to one and a half cakes for children from six to seven. Boys now began to help with work. They followed their fathers to market and carried bundles. Girls did some spinning at home.

At fifteen boys went to school. The sons of nobles and

the sons of commoners studied separately, but all of them dressed in black clothes, and they let their hair go uncut. Only the sons of nobles were allowed to learn reading and writing and understanding the calendar. Some of the commoners went to military schools. Others studied to be potters or weavers or craftsmen.

Girls were never taught any of these things in their schools. They spent their time learning how to weave and do fancy featherwork—and how to behave. They had to be modest and obedient and reverent. School for both girls and boys lasted till they were married.

GOD ON A STONE IN CACTUS

Young men who became craftsmen made beautiful objects of all kinds. Some of their work decorated the magnificent temples. Other things were for the splendid palaces and costumes of the nobles. Others were for merchants to use in trading with far-off places. Goldsmiths made delicate necklaces and jeweled nose-plugs, which Aztecs thought were as handsome as earrings.

Other skilled men wove cloth or painted pictures, or made lovely pottery, or mosaics into which they fitted tiny bits of sky-blue turquoise.

With all of this, plus the tribute that came from the conquered tribes, the Aztecs' capital city was a brilliant and busy place. They called it Tenochtitlan, which meant The Place Where the God Sits on a Stone in the Cactus, in honor of the sacred eagle, in the ancient prophecy.

Still another prophecy had been made by the priests. It was part of a whole legend about one of their gods, Quetzalcoatl, the Feathered Serpent. He was supposed to be white-skinned and bearded, with great wings. Long ago he had taught the Aztecs reading and writing and had driven off evil spirits. But there came a time when he went away toward the east. As he went, he said that he would return, and he gave them the exact year, according to the calendar.

Now a strange coincidence happened in the very year Quetzalcoatl was supposed to return. A white man with a beard came out of the East to the shores of Mexico in a ship with great white sails that looked like wings. With him were many other white, bearded men.

News of this wonder traveled quickly. Runners in relays carried word from the seacoast to the Aztec capital. The streets of the city filled with excited people. Had the prophecy of Quetzalcoatl's return come true? Montezuma, the Aztec's war chief, wondered, too. He sent great gifts of gold, hoping to make friends of the godlike strangers.

The white men were Spaniards, of course. Their leader was Hernando Cortes, and there was nothing in the world any of them loved more than gold. That was just what they had come to Mexico to get. Cortes began to make plans for a march on the Aztec capital. He found that many Indians would go with him, glad of a chance to overthrow the Aztecs who had conquered them and taken many of their people for human sacrifices. The Aztecs were feared but not loved by the millions over whom they ruled.

Cortes was amazed when he reached the Aztec capital. The causeways, the towering pyramids, the floating islands of flowers, and all the signs of great wealth seemed almost unbelievable.

The Spanish priests who came with Cortes were equally

amazed. But they were shocked by the idea of human sacrifice as a part of religion, although the killing of people who resisted their own beliefs seemed perfectly natural and right to them. For a while the Aztecs and the Spaniards argued about their different religious ideas. Finally the Aztecs gave their visitors a temple where the Spaniards could worship in their own way.

Then one day 600 Aztecs, mostly the noble leaders, gathered for ceremonies. They came unarmed, and they had promised not to make any sacrifices. In the midst of the ceremony, the fully armed Spaniards attacked the worshipers and killed every one of the 600.

Immediately the whole city rose against the Spaniards, and drove them out over the causeways. Many, loaded down with stolen gold, were captured and sacrificed.

With great luck and daring, Cortes and a few soldiers managed to fight their way through an Aztec army of 200,000. And in the end the Spaniards, with horses, artillery, muskets, armor, swords, and steel-bladed spears, conquered the whole of Mexico. The glories of the Maya, the Aztec, and the Toltec civilizations came to an end.

The Indians lost their chance to grow and develop in their own way. The Spanish even burned all of their learned books. The eyes of astronomers who had once looked at the stars were now turned toward the ground as they carried burdens for their conquerors on their backs. Soon no Indian remembered how to read or write, but the treasury of the faraway Spanish king was filled with Aztec gold.

CHAPTER 21

Ten Million Children of the Sun

THE RUNNER's chest heaved as he gulped the thin high-mountain air. He had come at breakneck speed for nearly two miles along the smooth-surfaced road. But just ahead he saw a shelter house. With an extra effort, he shouted.

Two men dashed out of the shelter. One snatched off his own warm mantle and pulled it across the sweat-covered back of the runner. The other tossed his cloak through the shelter doorway and listened carefully to the gasped-out message: "Atahualpa is the victor! Atahualpa is the Only Inca! Huascar, his brother, is defeated! Long live Atahualpa! Prepare for his visit!"

Instantly the listener was off down the road. Two miles ahead stood another thatched stone shelter house where he would speak the same message to another runner, who would pass it along to the next shelter.

In four short days, the news traveled north for twelve hundred miles through the heart of the Inca realm. One swift runner after another carried the words along the smooth highway that clung to the sides of steep mountains and crossed deep canyons on swinging bridges.

When a runner glanced down, he saw terraced farms in the beautiful valleys far below. Above him, along the sides of the peaks, herdsmen watched flocks of woolly llamas and long-haired alpacas. Soon news about the end of the civil war would spread to the farmers and the herdsmen. All would get ready to watch the triumphal procession of Atahualpa, the new Inca. To them, the Inca was ruler over the people in time of peace, commander of the armies, and a living god as well. (They called him the Only Inca. We call all the people he ruled the Incas.)

CIVIL WAR

Everyone knew what this civil war was about. Atahualpa and Huascar were brothers—sons of the old Inca who had ruled over ten million people. His realm stretched out for three thousand miles along the high Andes Mountains in South America. The two boys had grown up in different places—Atahualpa in the northern city of Quito and Huascar in the central capital at Cuzco. When the old Inca died, he named Huascar to take his place, and he made Atahualpa chief of the northern part of the country. But Atahualpa was ambitious—and more popular than his brother. He plotted a revolt against Huascar. And now his revolt had succeeded.

So Atahualpa would make his triumphal journey all through the marvelous Inca land. At the front of his procession walked men who cleaned weeds and loose stones from the road. Five thousand soldiers armed with slingshots marched next. Then came Atahualpa on a throne carried by the most important chiefs in the land. Over the throne rose two high golden arches in which precious stones were set. Curtains embroidered with the Inca's special insignia—the sun and moon and large serpents—hung down at the sides. No common person was ever supposed to look at the Inca, but he could peer out through holes in the curtains and see the throngs of people who came from their work and watched as he passed by.

At regular places along the roads stood inns where Atahualpa and his official wife and his half-sister and the high priest stopped at night. The procession moved slowly, no more than ten or twelve miles a day. At the inns, Atahualpa talked to local governors and gave the people a chance to bring up any complaints they had. Everything was orderly, everything was done according to rule, as the Inca's splendid procession moved on.

Now and then the marchers swayed hundreds of feet in the air on the swinging bridges that crossed chasms. Pairs of handmade ropes a foot thick stretched from one cliff to another and supported the roadbed made of branches and matting. Smaller ropes for handrails kept travelers from tumbling off. At one place, the road crossed a lake on a pontoon bridge.

CITY OF GOLD

At last the splendid city of Cuzco lay ahead. In the center stood the huge stone Temple of the Sun, entirely covered with a layer of gold. Inside the temple hung a great gold mirror, which reflected the sun as it rose in the morning. On the high priest's wrist was a silver mirror, polished and shaped like a saucer. At certain great ceremonies he caught the rays of the sun in the mirror, which focused them into a hot point as a magnifying glass does. With this mirror he started the ceremonial fire.

Water flowed to the fine temple fountains through pipes made of gold. Gardeners worked in the temple grounds with golden spades. Near by was an artificial garden in which all the trees and flowers were delicately molded of silver and gold. Even the cooks in the Inca's kitchen used golden pots and pans. There was more

An Inca market place

splendor in this American Indian city of Cuzco than in any other city in the world.

Gold by the ton lay piled in storehouses, but to the Incas it was not money. It was merely something beautiful and sacred to their god, the sun. They called it "the sun's tears." In fact, money was not useful to the Incas in the way it is to us. Their whole world was planned and worked out in a very special way.

QUICK FINGERS

Quick Fingers, the son of a weaver in the city of Cuzco, knew from the beginning what he was going to do when he was a man. Children always grew up to be the same things their fathers were. Meanwhile he was free to play with other children. He took part in sports and watched the many ceremonies and enjoyed the street life of the busy city. He peeked into shops where nobles were having jewels set in their teeth. He even caught glimpses of doctors at work setting broken bones, or prescribing quinine for fevers. One great surgeon, he knew, could operate on people's skulls and cut through the bone after they'd had special medicine to kill the pain.

When Quick Fingers was sixteen, he sat down at a weaving frame beside his father. Now he was in school, learning the weaver's trade. His fingers were very clever at passing the fine thread in and out among other threads with a kind of needle. Sometimes the cotton strands he used were finer than any that are made today. After four years of study and practice, he began to do a man's work. Already he had chosen a wife and was married. If he hadn't chosen her, the governor would have picked a wife for him when he was twenty-five, and neither he nor the girl would have had anything to say about it.

Until Quick Fingers was fifty years old, he raised his family and did his weaving in his own house. As his sons reached sixteen, he taught them the trade. After that he began to make journeys to distant parts of the country. He was a full-time teacher of weaving now, and he gave his skill to men of far-off tribes who had recently been conquered by the Inca armies.

When he was sixty years old, Quick Fingers retired. All his life he had worked for the government and had received as pay a place in which to live and the food and clothing that he and his family needed. After he retired, he kept on getting these things.

Because he was a skilled craftsman, Quick Fingers had never been drafted into the army, as farmers were. They had to spend part of their time as soldiers, or in work crews on highways or other great building projects. When young farmers lived near the roads, they took turns being runners on the sections of the highway nearest their homes. Two at a time, they lived in the shelter houses, waiting to speed messages through the country.

Some young men took turns at smoke-signal stations, too. They could send urgent messages even faster than runners carried them. News traveled by smoke signals all over the vast Inca country in a very few hours.

High in the mountains lived the families of miners who did the special work of digging gold, silver, and copper from the earth. Without explosives or steel tools, they hammered the precious ores out of the mountainsides. The governors took great care to make sure the miners did not work too long or too hard at their dangerous jobs.

All this careful planning for the whole country was possible because the governors kept exact count of all the people and the food they grew and the things they made. And the bookkeepers did this without ever writing numbers down on a piece of paper! All Inca figuring was done with knots in strings of different colors. Small pieces of string hung like a fringe from a main string. By looking at the colors of the string, the knots, and where they were tied, a man could tell the numbers it represented.

These string adding machines were called quipus, and only the nobles went to schools where they learned how to do quipu arithmetic. They learned all about government in their schools, too. Government for the Incas wasn't just a matter of orders. It took a great deal of thinking and planning. Young nobles had to know where each kind of crop would grow best. They had to plan out caravans that traveled along the highways carrying food or cloth or gold from the places where things were produced to places where they were needed. They figured carefully so that food was stored up for times of drought. They supervised the farming.

The governors made sure that every farmer had his fair share of water from irrigation ditches. They saw to it that no one starved or lacked clothes and a house to live in. In return, everyone had to do his fair share of the work. The Inca commoners were poor, but not so poor that they wanted to revolt against the nobles. When Atahualpa overthrew his brother Huascar and became the Only Inca, the people who took his side were only changing one Inca for another who was more popular.

But the civil war did divide the country and leave it weaker. And by chance at just that moment 200 Spaniards sailed up the coast of South America, led by a cruel and treacherous man named Pizarro, looking for gold.

The Spaniards had arms and horses, just as Cortes's men had in Mexico. The Incas, like the Aztecs, were frightened at the strange animals and the guns. They, too, had a prophecy that white men would some day come and rule over them.

Word reached Atahualpa that the white men were marching up the mountain valleys, but he did nothing to stop them. How could he stop something that a sacred prophecy said was bound to happen? Atahualpa could have sent 200,000 men against Pizarro's 200. He could have destroyed them instantly. Instead, he thought it was best to make friends with the invaders.

THE GREAT BETRAYAL

And so Atahualpa met Pizarro in the square of the city called Caxamarca. Around the Inca stood thousands of his followers, who had come unarmed to receive the strange white men. Pizarro saw his advantage. Then and there, the well-armed Spaniards killed many thousands of defenseless Indians, and they made a prisoner of Atahualpa, who was the Indians' ruler and god.

Now Pizarro promised to let Atahualpa go free in exchange for a room full of gold and two rooms full of silver. The Incas paid the ransom, but instead of freeing Atahualpa, Pizarro killed him.

The Incas were so terrified that they let the Spaniards

steal whatever they wanted. The conquerors stripped the gold from the temples. They took every bit of gold and silver from the homes of the nobles and sent the people into the mines as slaves to dig still more. They destroyed storehouses, let bridges fall into the canyons, butchered the flocks, and tore down buildings. Although a new Inca appeared and led a long fight against the Spaniards, the Indians were not able to save the wonderful civilization they had built up.

In a few years, the work of many centuries was wiped from the earth. The Spaniards took complete control of all but the most distant points. There for a long time Indians kept on fighting for independence.

An Inca city in the mountains

CHAPTER 22

Hiawatha's United States

ALTHOUGH the Indians in ancient Peru were ruled by the Inca and the nobles, the common people had many democratic rights. There were regular ways for them to complain about bad officials and to get good officials in their place. They were always sure of food and clothing and shelter. The work was divided up fairly.

As a matter of fact there was a great deal of democracy everywhere among the Indians. In most tribes the people themselves were really the rulers. The chiefs didn't inherit their jobs the way kings do, and the people chose new chiefs when they thought the old ones weren't being good leaders. In most tribes women and men were equals. They just had different kinds of work to do. And almost everywhere children were treated with great kindness. They weren't just ordered around. That was democratic, too.

EVERYBODY'S LAND

Most important of all, the farmers and hunters owned their own lands or hunting grounds. They owned them all together, and very often they farmed and hunted together for the good of all.

The Indians liked their way of life and they fought hard to keep it when white men from the outside started to order them around. In a few places rich rulers like

Montezuma and Atahualpa surrendered easily. So did the fishing Indians of the Northwest coast. And here is an interesting thing. These Indians were much more concerned about wealth and possessions than they were about independence. Food was so plentiful that not everybody had to work. Some men could grow rich and powerful enough to make others fish and hunt for them. The fishing Indians had many slaves. So did the Aztec nobles, and they ruled by making people fear them instead of talking things over and reaching an agreement. When the white men attacked, the slaves had very little to lose anyway, so they did not resist.

But the Indian people as a whole fought hard for their independence for four hundred years. Some of the tribes that put up the greatest fights were the most democratic—tribes like the Apaches and the Sioux. The Iroquois tribes in New York State put up one of the strongest battles of all. They could do this because they had a government that was more carefully planned than any other among the Indians in North America.

Old men in the Iroquois tribes used to tell the story of Hiawatha to explain how their government got started.

TOO MUCH WAR

This Hiawatha, who was not the one in Longfellow's poem, lived long before the white men came. A lot of legends about him got mixed up with facts, of course. But one thing was sure. The Iroquois honored Hiawatha because he had brought peace among them.

Hiawatha belonged to the Onondaga tribe. His people were always at war with their cousins—the Senecas, the Mohawks, the Cayugas, and the Oneidas. Like almost all tribes, they began their quarrel over the right to use certain hunting grounds. But long after the quarrel was settled, the fighting kept on, like a bad habit.

When Hiawatha was a young man, he accepted the war customs that all the tribes had. Silent, swift-running scouts from the Onondagas would steal into a Mohawk village and leave a red tomahawk in front of the Long House. This was a warning and a challenge to war.

But as Hiawatha grew older, he realized that the wars were of no real use to anyone, and he thought of a plan to stop them. If his own tribe, which was the strongest, offered peace to all its neighbors, this would be a good beginning. Then gradually treaties of peace could spread out and take in more and more tribes. Finally there could be peace everywhere.

So Hiawatha took his plan to the chief of his tribe, Atotarho, the Tangled One, a warrior who showed his magic power by having snakes instead of hair growing from his head.

Atotarho wasn't sure the plan would work. All the other Onondaga chiefs were doubtful too. The idea was too new for them.

THE JOURNEY FOR PEACE

So Hiawatha set out on a great journey, hoping to win over the chiefs of neighboring tribes. Traveling alone, he walked along forest trails and climbed mountains. He crossed lakes and floated down dangerous rivers in a canoe. Finally he reached the town of a Cayuga chief named Dekanawidah, who, he believed, would be friendly.

There Hiawatha sat on a log by a spring waiting for

someone to see him. A woman came for water and ran to the chief saying, "A man whose breast is covered with white shells is seated at the spring."

The chief heard this and said to one of his brothers, "It is a guest. Go and bring him in. We will make him welcome."

Now Hiawatha had won his first success. The Cayugas had invited him to their village as a guest. He would have a chance to speak and he would be listened to.

Hiawatha loved to make speeches about peace. He made such a beautiful one that he convinced Dekanawidah, whose name meant "Two Rivers Meeting." The Cayuga chief liked the idea of having all the tribes meet like rivers flowing together. Soon the Cayugas were for Hiawatha's united-nations plan.

Now Dekanawidah helped Hiawatha win over the Mohawks and the Oneidas and the Senecas. Finally they worked out a way of convincing Hiawatha's own people, the Onondagas, and the warrior chief Atotarho.

COUNCIL OF SACHEMS

In order to keep peace among the different tribes, they would set up a council of fifty sachems, or wise men, over them all. The most honored place in the council would go to the Onondagas. They would have fourteen of the fifty sachems.

The council would discuss any arguments or problems that came up between the tribes. They would figure out how to get other tribes to sign peace treaties with them. Discussions would go on until all the sachems agreed. Every decision had to be unanimous. (It is the same with decisions in the Security Council of the United

Nations today!) In this way, no tribe could ever get the feeling that it was being pushed around by the other tribes, and all would remain loyal to each other.

At last Hiawatha and Dekanawidah presented the whole plan to Atotarho. The Onondagas joined in the Iroquois League, and Atotarho became as great a leader for peace as he had been in war.

MAN WHO COMBS

Every member of the council got a special name when he became a sachem. This is how the names came about: Runners went out over the trails, looking for the fifty men who had been chosen. The runners had been told to notice anything special about the new sachems at the moment they saw them. One man was picking dry fluffy cattails. So the runner named him Man Covered with Cattail Down. Another man was hanging up the rattles he used in dances. His name became Hanging Up Rattles. Another became Small Speech, because he said very little when he heard the news. Others were Man Steaming Himself, Man with a Headache.

And it was only now that Hiawatha got the name by which he is remembered. The runner came up to him just as he was combing his hair, with news that he had been chosen sachem. Hiawatha means Man Who Combs.

Most sachems kept their jobs as long as they lived. When a sachem died, his name was passed on to someone else elected to the council by his clan.

The names lived on, and so did the work of keeping peace and spreading it. The League of Five Nations offered membership to neighboring tribes. The Iroquois said, "You may join as equals and have peace—or the same old war will go on." The Tuscaroras, who came from far-off North Carolina and Virginia, accepted the offer. They became the sixth tribe in the League, and they moved to New York State.

Other tribes chose war instead of peace. Many of them were defeated and almost destroyed in wars against the Iroquois. The few remaining members of some of these tribes finally accepted protection in the League.

For two hundred years the League grew, and the Iroquois pushed war farther and farther away from the big, bark-covered houses in their towns.

The League of Six Nations itself might still endure today if Americans had kept their treaties with these Indians, and if Englishmen, pretending to be their friends, hadn't paid them well for bringing in American scalps at the time of the Revolution.

Even so, the Iroquois League lives today in a very important way that few people realize. Some of the Indian ideas of democratic government are in our own United States Constitution.

Yes, that's right. Remember that the Constitution was written at a time when every American knew about the strength of the tribes that had united in the League, and many Americans knew at first hand how the Iroquois democracy worked. Right on their own borders the Thirteen Colonies had a very good model for unity and fairness and co-operation. Seeking their own independence, Americans found good freedom-ideas that had already grown up on American soil.

CHAPTER 23

Indians and You

STORIES about Indians are very exciting to read, but perhaps you may be thinking that they are all very far away and long ago.

The fact is—your life would be very different if there had never been any Indians. Listen to this:

More than half of all the grain and vegetables and fruit grown on American farms comes from plants the Indians discovered and developed. Besides corn, Indians discovered white potatoes, sweet potatoes, beans, peanuts, tomatoes, pumpkins, cocoa, tobacco, cranberries and many other berries, maple sugar, hickory and Brazil nuts, pears, peppers, pineapple, tapioca, vanilla, American cotton, and rubber.

Indians gave these medicines to doctors: quinine, cocaine, cascara sagrada, ipecac, witch hazel, oil of wintergreen, arnica, and many drugs from herbs.

These Indian inventions are still widely used: moccasins, canoes, hammocks, tepees, pack baskets, toboggans, snow goggles, snowshoes.

And where would sports be if the Indians hadn't invented rubber balls? There is rubber in the balls with which we play tennis, baseball, basketball, and golf.

But that's not the end. Tribes all over played lacrosse, a popular sport today that is Canada's national game.

Most important of all the things we borrowed from

the Indians is corn. More land is used for growing it than for growing any other crop. Hogs, cows, chickens, horses, sheep, eat four-fifths of all the corn that is raised. So every time you have a slice of bacon or an egg or a mutton chop or a glass of milk, you are enjoying some of the marvelous grain that Indians created.

It would take many pages to list all the uses for corn, besides the ones you can think of without half trying. Here are a few of the many things that have corn products in them: puddings, salad dressing, sausage, scrapple, yeast, ice cream, talcum powder, tooth paste, margarine, nail-polish remover, perfume, paper, crayons, ink, glue, oilcloth, soaps, twine, window shades, rayon, antifreeze, and dope for model airplanes.

Add chewing gum to the list of Indian contributions, too.

Even the expression "OK" is Indian. It's from the Choctaw language.

Many of the things that Boy Scouts, Girl Scouts, and Girl Guides do are based on Indian lore. In fact, a great Indian, Charles Eastman, helped start the Boy Scouts.

Whenever you take a long trip, you are almost sure to travel over an old Indian trail. Many important roads and railroads have been built following exactly where Indians' feet first marked the best route.

Indians, and what they have done, are a very important part of American life.

Every year that goes by, Indians become more important. Now that redskin and paleface live peacefully side by side, the Indians are no longer a dying people. Instead they are the fastest growing part of the American population. About 400,000 Indians live in the United

Modern Mayas

States today. In thirty years there will be as many as there were when white men first came.

Indians are citizens just the same as anybody else. A law giving them citizenship was passed in 1924. After that Indians could vote in most states. In 1948 they won the right to vote in Arizona and New Mexico. However, there are still special laws in some Southern states that make it difficult for Indians, as well as Negroes, to vote.

Indians don't have to stay on reservations, but about two-thirds of them do. One reason is that they find it hard to make a living elsewhere. Even if they do get good jobs, they often cannot live as equals among whites. In many places laws and customs keep them apart from white Americans. On the reservation they are among their own people and they have homes and land that cannot be bought away from them.

THE INDIAN SERVICE

A special branch of the government has the job of helping Indians improve their life on reservations. It is the United States Indian Service of the Department of the Interior. The Indian Service runs schools. It has nurses, doctors, and hospitals. It teaches modern farming methods, arranges loans for improvements, and does many other such things.

Half of the people who work for the Indian Service are Indians, and several reservations now have Indian superintendents. But the Indian Service does not get nearly enough money to do all that needs to be done if Indians are to have the same advantages as other Americans. For instance, there are no schools at all for 20,000 Navaho children. There aren't nearly enough hospitals on reservations, either, or doctors or nurses or dentists. Indians have a great deal of sickness because so many of them are poor. Most of them live on the worst land in the United States. And even when there are good new ways to make a living, Indians cannot always use the new ideas quickly. For instance, in some tribes women always did the farm work, while men did the hunting and fighting. This has always seemed right and natural to them. Now suppose that one of these tribes has to settle down on farm land, with tractors and farm machinery. Hunting and fighting are things of the past. Tractors and machines seem very strange to them, and strangest of all is the idea that *men* should do *any* farm work.

This is only one example of the things that make it hard for Indians to fit into the modern world quickly. There is a special reason why some Indians keep old ideas that interfere with change. Those ideas seem like trusted friends—and there is not much friendship in the world that asks them to give up their old ways.

But not all tribes are poor, of course. For instance, the Menominees in Wisconsin own a prosperous sawmill where they cut up timber from their own land. The Jicarilla Apache reservation in New Mexico has good grazing land, and the people there get along well as ranchers. The Flathead Indians in Montana also make a good living from grazing lands, and they are paid for electric power that is made at a dam on their land. Some Osage Indians in Oklahoma are very rich indeed. They get their money from oil under their land.

While farming is the work of most Indians today, many Pueblos sell their beautiful pottery, and some Navahos sell their lovely blankets and silver jewelry. And Indians all over work at lots of other jobs too. For instance, about 500 Mohawks live far from their reservation—in Brooklyn, New York. They are expert bridge builders, and they have helped put up some of the highest skyscrapers.

INDIANS AND THE FUTURE

Indians don't just sit on reservations and wait for help. They are helping themselves. They have their own organizations—dozens of them—besides their tribes. Most of these protect the rights of Indians and work in some way or other to make a better life for the original Americans. Two of the most important of these organizations are the Indian Council Fire in Chicago and the National Congress of American Indians, which has headquarters in Washington and tries to get Congress to pass laws the Indians need.

In many ways the growing number of Indians in our country are saying, "We who have already given a great deal to American life are determined to give a great deal more."

Indians Where You Live

INDIANS have lived everywhere in the United States. Your own home town may have been an Indian town long ago. Many cities, states, rivers, and mountains have interesting Indian names. In the next pages you will find some of these place names and what they mean. Look up your own state and you will find most of the important tribes who have lived there in the past, together with most important groups of Indians who live there today.

Tribes often lived in several different states, or moved from one state to another. When they are listed under one state, it doesn't always mean that this is the only place they have lived.

ALASKA (Territory)

Alaska is the Eskimo word for "peninsula." Indians gave Eskimos their name, which means "people who eat their meat raw."

Tribes in the past: Eskimo, Aleut, Athabascan, Tlingit, Tsimshian, Haida.

Now: The same, but fewer in number.

ALABAMA

Alabama means "I clear away the thicket." The state was named after the Alabama tribe of Indians who once lived there.

Tribes in the past: Mound Builder, Alabama, Creek, Cherokee, Choctaw, and Yuchi.

Now: Except for a few Creeks near Atmore, no tribes live here today. The Alabamas live in Texas and in Oklahoma.

Names: Tuscaloosa means "Black Warrior," the name of a chief. Mobile is an ancient Indian name for one of their towns.

ARIZONA

Arizona may be named after an Indian word that means "silver-bearing."

Tribes in the past: Navaho, Apache, Hopi, Mojave, Havasupai, Hualapai, Chemehuevi, Maricopa, Paiute, Papago, Pima.

Now: These same tribes live just about where they have lived for hundreds of years, except that their reservations are smaller than their former lands. Many Yaqui Indians have moved from Mexico to Arizona in the last fifty years.

Names: Tucson means "black creek." Navaho comes from the Tewa and means "large cornfield." The Apaches got their name from the neighboring Zuni Indians; it means "enemy." Hopi means "peaceful ones" in the Hopi language. Cochise is named for a famous Apache chief.

ARKANSAS

Arkansas is the way white men spelled "Acansea," the name of a tribe who lived there. Another name for this tribe was "Quapaw."

Tribes in the past: Mound Builder, Caddo, Miami, Osage, Quapaw, Cherokee (for a few years).

Now: No tribes. All former inhabitants live in Oklahoma.

Names: Osceola was named for a famous Seminole chief who led his people in a war for independence. Pocahontas was named for the Powhatan Indian girl in Virginia who was supposed to have saved the life of Captain John Smith.

CALIFORNIA

Tribes in the past: Some tribes in southern California were held almost as slaves by the Spanish missions. They are often grouped together under the name Mission Indians. Some of them are: Cahuilla, Luiseno, Chumash. Other tribes were called Diggers because, instead of farming, they dug up wild roots and other food from the earth. Maidus and Modocs were Diggers. Still other tribes were: Hupa, Pomo, Yuma, Yurok.

Now: All these tribes live on sixteen reservations near their original homes or in ninety-nine rancherias, which are little collections of huts.

Names: Tulare means "place of reeds." Ojai means "west." Modoc means "southerners." Tehama means "high water." Napa means "city" or "house."

COLORADO

Tribes in the past: Folsom Man, Basket Maker, Cliff Dweller, Ute, Arapahoe, Cheyenne.

Now: The Ute Reservation is in the southwestern part of the state. The Cliff Dwellers moved and joined the Pueblos in New Mexico. Arapahoes and Cheyennes live in Oklahoma and Wyoming today.

Names: Manitou means "Great Spirit." Saguache means "water on the blue earth." Left Hand Creek gets its name from an Arapahoe chief named Left Hand. Ouray is named for a great Ute chief.

CONNECTICUT

Connecticut means "the river whose water is driven in waves by tides or winds."

Tribes in the past: Pequot.

Now: A few Pequots still live here.

Names: Higganum means "at the tomahawk rock." Housatonic is "the proud river flowing through the rocks." Willimantic means "good lookout."

DELAWARE

Tribes in the past: Delaware Indians called themselves Leni-Lenape, meaning "real men."

Now: No tribes. The Delawares now live in Oklahoma and Kansas, but a group of people in the state called "Moors" are probably partly descended from the Nanticoke tribe of Delawares, and so are a group of people living on Indian River.

Names: Nanticoke River is named for the tribe and means "the tidewater people."

FLORIDA

Tribes in the past: Mound Builder, Calusa, Timucua, Seminole (Creeks who came from the North), Apalachee.

Now: Seminoles. Many Calusas moved to Cuba. The Apalachees joined the Creeks and other tribes.

Names: Seminole means "runaway." Lake Okeechobee means "large water." Tallahassee means "old town." Tampa means "close to it." Pensacola means "hair people." The Appalachian

Mountains to the north were named for the Apalachees by the first Spanish explorers.

GEORGIA

Tribes in the past: Mound Builder, Creek, Yuchi, Cherokee.

Now: No tribes. The Creeks and Yuchis now live in Oklahoma, Texas, and Louisiana. The Cherokees live mainly in Oklahoma, but have a reservation in North Carolina.

Names: The English settlers named the Creeks for the large number of streams or creeks in their territory. The Creeks called themselves Muskogee, meaning "swamp." Savannah is the way the Creek Indians pronounced "Shawnee," the name of another tribe meaning "southerners." Chattahoochee means "painted stone." Tallapoosa means "swift current." Unadilla is "meeting place." Hightower is an English mispronunciation of Etowah, the name of an old Cherokee town.

IDAHO

Idaho is an Indian word, but its meaning has been forgotten.

Tribes in the past: Bannock, Shoshone, Nez Percé, Cœur d'Alêne.

Now: The same. Their reservations are in about the same places where they have always lived.

Names: Bannock means "southern people." Nez Percé is French for "pierced nose." The name comes from the tribe's custom of wearing decorations in their noses. Cœur d'Alêne means "needle heart" in French. The name refers to the sharp bargaining that went on between the Indians and the French traders.

ILLINOIS

Illinois means "men." It was the name for a group of tribes who had treaties with each other and formed a league.

Tribes in the past: Mound Builder; Cahokia, Kaskaskia, Peoria (these three were part of the Illinois League).

Now: No tribes. Members of the Illinois League now live in Oklahoma.

Names: Peoria means "carriers." Chicago is "wild-onion place"—in other words, a place with a bad smell! Winnetka is "beautiful place."

INDIANA

Indiana got its name from the word "Indian."

Tribes in the past: Mound Builders, Miami. Also a large band of Delawares called Munsees, which means "at the place where the stones are gathered together," lived in Indiana for a while after they moved out of the East.

Now: A few years ago only four full-blood Miamis still lived in the state. The rest of the tribe lives in Oklahoma.

Names: Muncie is another way of spelling Munsee. The city is named for the Munsee band of Delawares. Wabash means "cloud borne by a wind." Mishawaka is the way white people pronounced the name of a famous Miami chief. It means "little turtle."

IOWA

Iowa gets its name from an Indian tribe. It means "sleepy ones."

Tribes in the past: Mound Builder, Iowa. Also part of the Sauk and Fox tribes. Sauk means "people living at a river mouth." Fox was what white men called the whole tribe, using the English name of one of its bands. Fox Indians called themselves "Red Earth People."

Now: Several hundred Sauk-Foxes live on a reservation near Tama. The rest of the tribe live in Kansas and Oklahoma, and the Iowas all live in Nebraska, Kansas, and Oklahoma.

Names: Council Bluffs got its name from a council that the explorers Lewis and Clark held there with the Indians. Sioux City was named for the famous plains tribe. Sioux means "enemy" in Chippewa. The grave of a famous Sauk chief, Keokuk, meaning "one who moves about alertly," is in the city named for him. Ottumwa means "tumbling water."

KANSAS

Kansas got its name from a local tribe, the Kansa (or Kaw) Indians.

Tribes in the past: Mound Builder, Osage, Apache, Kansa, Pawnee, and Kiowa. Shawnees also lived in Kansas for a while before going to Oklahoma.

Now: Sauk-Foxes, Iowas, Kickapoos and Potawatomis. Haskell Institute, an important Indian school, is in Kansas.

Names: Wichita takes its name from a Texas tribe of Indians. Topeka is an Indian name for potato. Osawatomie is a combination of the words Osage and Potawatomi. Chetopa is "four houses." The town was built where four houses belonging to an Osage chief once stood.

KENTUCKY

Kentucky is an Indian word, but its meaning is not known.

Tribes in the past: Mound Builders, Shawnees (meaning "southerners"). Many other tribes used the state for hunting grounds.

Now: No tribes.

Names: An Indian chief is buried on the banks of the Tennessee River at Paducah, which bears his name.

LOUISIANA

Tribes in the past: Mound Builder, Chitimacha, Natchez, Washa Chawasha, Tunica, Caddo, and Attacapa.

Now: About 150 Chitimachas live on their own reservation. Several hundred people, partly of Indian descent, who call themselves Houma Indians live near Houma. They are not organized into a tribe. Neither are the Cajuns, who are a group also having Indian ancestors. Some Choctaws, Koasatis and Tunicas live here.

Names: Opelousas means "black haired." Houma means "red."

MAINE

Tribes in the past: Abnaki, meaning "people of the east," was the name given to a whole group of tribes that lived in Maine.

Now: Three of the Abnaki tribes, the Passamaquoddy, Malecite and the Penobscot, still live in the state. There are also some Micmacs.

Names: Kennebec and Kennebunk mean "long watering place" or "long lake." Mt. Katahdin is "highest land." Madawaska is "porcupine place." Millinocket is "place full of islands." Skowhegan is "watching place." Wiscasset is "place of the yellow pine." Old Town gets its name because an old Indian town once stood there. Norridgewock is "place of deer."

MARYLAND

Tribes in the past: Conoy (or Kanawha), Piscataway, and Nanticoke.

Now: No tribes.

Names: Chesapeake Bay is the "great salty bay." Pocomoke means "broken by knolls." Takoma Park means "mountain park." Piscataway is named for the tribe.

MASSACHUSETTS

Massachusetts means "near the great hills."

Tribes in the past: White men called one of the tribes in the western part of the state the Stockbridge Indians. An Indian name for them was Housatonic, which means "proud river flowing through the rocks." The Massachusetts tribe lived in the eastern part of the state. The Indians the Pilgrims found were Wampanoags.

Now: Some descendants of the Massachusetts and Wampanoags live on Cape Cod and on Martha's Vineyard.

Names: Agawam means "marsh." Chicopee is "cedar river." Cochituate is "land on rapid streams." Nahant means "two things united." Saugus is a word for "extended." Scituate is "cold brook." Swampscott is "broken waters."

MICHIGAN

Michigan means "big lake."

Tribes in the past: Menominees ("wild rice people") and Potawatomis ("firemakers"). Also the Erie (or "wildcat") and Neutral tribes lived in the southeast corner of the state.

Now: Chippewa Indians live on the L'Anse and Isabella reservations and Ottawas live on Beaver Island in Lake Michigan.

Names: Algonac means "land of the people who spear fish and eels from the bow of a canoe." Sheboygan is named for the "river that comes out of the ground." Kalamazoo is a word for "otter tail." Otsego is "place where meetings are held." Pontiac is named for a famous Ottawa chief. Sandusky means "there is pure water here." Saginaw is a Chippewa word for "Sauk place." Wyandotte is named for a tribe. Owosso was the name of a Chippewa chief, meaning "he is far off."

MINNESOTA

Minnesota is a Sioux word for "sky-colored water."

Tribes in the past: Mound Builders, the Santee Dakota band of Sioux (or Dakota), Chippewa (or Ojibway).

Now: There are several large and a number of small Chippewa reservations. Sioux Indians live in four different places.

Names: Minneapolis is a combination of an Indian word meaning "water" and a Greek word meaning "city." Sauk Center was named for the tribe. Sleepy Eye was the name of a chief, and so was Wabasha, which is Sioux for "red cap." Winona is a Sioux word meaning "first-born daughter." And Pipestone gets its name from the red stone near by, which the Indians quarried and used for making pipes.

MISSISSIPPI

Mississippi means "gathering in all of the waters."

Tribes in the past: Mound Builder, Biloxi, Tunica, Ofogoula, and Choctaw.

Now: More than 2000 Choctaws live here.

Names: Pascagoula gets its name from an Indian band and means "bread people." Pontotoc was the name of a Chickasaw chief; it means "weed prairie." Okolona is a word for "much bent." The Tombigbee River gets its name from a word meaning "coffin makers." Biloxi means "first people."

MISSOURI

Missouri gets its name from a tribe; it means "muddy water."

Tribes in the past: Mound Builder, Missouri, Illinois, and Osage.

Now: No tribes.

Names: Chillicothe was the name of part of the Shawnee tribe and means "man made perfect." Neosho is "clear, cold water." Osceola was the name of a Seminole chief who led his people in a war for their independence from the whites. Sarcoxie was a chief who was friendly to the whites. Tarkio means "difficult to ford."

MONTANA

Tribes in the past: Crow, Atsina (or Gros Ventre), Shoshone, Assiniboin, Blackfoot, Piegan, Flathead, and Kootenai.

Now: Assiniboins, Blackfeet, Piegans, Chippewas, Crees, Gros Ventres, Sioux, Cheyennes, and Crows have reservations here.

Names: Missoula is a Salish word and means "by chilling waters." Assiniboin means "one who cooks by the use of stoves." Chippewa (or Ojibway) means "to roast until puckered up." Atsina means "gut people." Gros Ventres is French for "big bellies." Flathead Indians tied children's heads to cradle boards to make them flat.

NEBRASKA

Nebraska means "shallow water."

Tribes in the past: Mound Builder, Pawnee, Cheyenne, Oto, Omaha, Arikara, and Sioux.

Now: Iowas, Omahas, Winnebagos, Santee Sioux, and Poncas live here on reservations.

Names: Arapahoe is named for the tribe and means "traders." Oglalla is a Sioux band and refers to scattering. Red Cloud is the name of a Sioux chief. Wahoo is a kind of elm tree.

NEVADA

Tribes in the past: Shoshone, Paiute, Washo, and Goshute.

Now: These same tribes live on reservations.

Names: Winnemucca was a Paiute chief. Tahoe means "big water."

NEW HAMPSHIRE

Tribes in the past: Penacook.

Now: No tribes.

Names: Merrimack means "swift water." Nashua is "land between." Ossippee is "pine river." Penacook means "crooked." Sunapee is "wild-goose pond." And Suncook is "goose place."

NEW JERSEY

Tribes in the past: Delawares or Leni-Lenapes.

Now: No tribes, but a group of people in the northern part of the state who are called Jackson Whites are said to have some Indian blood.

Names: Hoboken means "tobacco pipe." Hopatcong means "stone over water." Manasquan is "point" or "top." Passaic is the way

Indians pronounced the English word "peace." Totowa means "to sink or go under the water as timbers do over a fall." Hackensack is "land of the big snake." Matawan is "magician." Metuchen was a chief of the Raritan band of Indians. Rahway means "in the middle of the forest." Raritan is "forked river." Secaucus means "snaky." Amboy means "hollow inside" or "like a bowl." Weehawken is "maize land."

NEW MEXICO

Tribes in the past: Sandia Man, Folsom Man, Basket Maker, Navaho, Apache, and many different tribes of Pueblo Indians.

Now: Navaho and Apache tribes live here on reservations, and Pueblos live in their old towns.

Names: Taos, Zuni, Tesuque, Cochiti, Jemez and Acoma are towns or pueblos that have their original Indian names.

NEW YORK

Tribes in the past: Montauk on Long Island, Wappinger and Mohican farther north along the Hudson. Mohawk, Oneida, Onondaga, Cayuga, and Seneca, all members of the Iroquois League, lived in the state, and so did the Tuscaroras after they joined the League.

Now: Senecas live on the Cattaraugus Reservation; Tuscaroras and Onondagas live on the Tuscarora Reservation; Senecas and Cayugas live on the Tonawanda Reservation; Mohawks on the St. Regis Reservation; and Onondagas, Oneidas and Cayugas live on the Onondaga Reservation. The Syossets and other groups live on Long Island.

Names: Canajoharie is "kettle that washes itself." Canandaigua is "chosen spot." Cattaraugus is "bad-smelling shore." Cohoes is "shipwrecked canoe." Coxsackie means "to cut the earth" and describes a ridge that the Hudson River cuts through. Katonah is the name of a chief and means "sickly." Mohawk means "eater of live bear meat." Nyack is "corner" or "point." Oneida means "granite people." Oneonta is "place of rest." Ossining is "place of stones." Oswego is "the valley widens." Patchogue is "turning place." Poughkeepsie is "safe harbor." Saranac is "river that flows under a rock." Saratoga Springs is "place of miraculous water in a rock." Sag Harbor is the harbor near which "ground nuts grow." Schenectady is "river valley beyond the pine trees." Skaneateles is "long lake." Ticonderoga is "noisy water." Tonawanda is "swift water." Niagara means "across the neck."

NORTH CAROLINA

Tribes in the past: Tuscarora, Weapemeoc, Secotan, Coree, Saponi, Cherokee, Cape Fear Indians.

Now: Only a small part of the Cherokees still live here.

Names: The Roanoke River gets its name from a kind of shell used for money. Lake Waccamaw is named for an Indian tribe.

NORTH DAKOTA

Dakota is a Sioux word meaning "allies."

Tribes in the past: Mandan, Dakota or Sioux, Arikara, Assiniboin, Chippewa, Hidatsa.

Now: Mandans, Hidatsas, Arikaras, Gros Ventres, Sioux, Chippewas, Assiniboins.

Names: Wahpeton is named for one of the Sioux tribes and means "leaf village." Mandan gets its name from the tribe.

OHIO

Ohio is "beautiful river."

Tribes in the past: Mound Builder. Three hundred years ago a tribe called the Erie, which means "long tailed like a panther," or "cat nation," lived here. After a war with the Iroquois the tribe disappeared, with many of its members joining the Iroquois League. Miamis also lived in Ohio. Delawares and other Indians forced to move out of the East lived in Ohio for a while.

Now: No tribes.

Names: Ashtabula is "fish river." Chillicothe is a Shawnee word for "man made perfect." Conneaut means "it is a long time since they are gone." Cuyahoga is a word for "crooked." Maumee is another form of Miami. Mingo was the name given to Iroquois living outside the Iroquois country, and means "spring people." Sandusky means "there is pure water here." Tippecanoe is a word for "at the great clearing." Toronto is "oak tree rising from the lake." The Scioto River is the "great legs" river because it has many branches.

OKLAHOMA

Oklahoma is a Choctaw word for "red people."

Tribes of the past: Kiowa, Caddo, and Osage.

Now: Oklahoma has the largest Indian population of any state, because many tribes were moved out of the East and put on reservations here. Before Oklahoma became a state, it was called Indian Territory. Among the tribes that live here now are: Cheyenne, Arapahoe, Kiowa, Wichita, Potawatomi, Shawnee, Sauk-Fox, Oto, Kaw (or Kansa), Osage, Quapaw, Peoria, Miami, Ottawa, Modoc, Wyandotte, Seneca, and what are called the Five Civilized Tribes—Cherokee, Creek, Choctaw, Chickasaw and Seminole.

Names: Towns are named after many of these and other tribes. Eufaula is the name of a Creek Indian town. Hominy is the name of one of the Indian ways of preparing corn. Tishomingo is named for a Chickasaw chief. Wewoka is "barking water."

OREGON

Tribes in the past: Paiute, Cayuse, Nez Percé, Tenno, Klamath, Tahelma, Kus, Yaquina, Kalapuya, Molala, Tillamook.

Now: Fragments of most of these tribes and of some others live on the Klamath, Warm Springs, Grande Ronde-Siletz, and Umatilla reservations.

Names: At one time the Cayuse Indians captured and sold so many wild horses that the word "cayuse" came to be used in the Northwest for any wild horse. Klamath means "the encamped."

PENNSYLVANIA

Tribes in the past: Mound Builder, Conestoga (or Susquehanna), Delaware (or Leni-Lenape).

Now: A few Senecas live on the Cornplanter Reservation near the northern border of the state.

Names: Conestoga was the name of the famous covered wagon made in Pennsylvania that pioneers used to cross the plains. Aliquippa was the name of a Delaware woman and means "hat." Conshohocken is "pleasant valley." Mauch Chunk is "bear mountain." Juniata means "they stay long." Kittanning is "greatest river." The Monongahela is "river with the sliding banks." Punxsutawney is "sand-fly place." Sewickley is "sweet water." Shamokin is a Delaware word meaning "place of eels." The Shenandoah is "sprucy stream." Shickshinny means "five mountains." Susquehanna means "water." Wyoming is "large plains."

RHODE ISLAND

Tribes in the past: Narragansett.

Now: A few Narragansetts are organized together and own two acres of land.

Names: Narragansett means "people of the point." Natick is "place of the hills." Pascoag is "dividing place." Pawtucket means "at the little falls." Scituate is "cold brook." Woonsocket is "at the place of mist."

SOUTH CAROLINA

Tribes in the past: Cherokee, Yuchi, Catawba, Sewee, Cheraw, Shawnee, and Cusabo.

Now: Catawbas live on a reservation near Rock Hill.

Names: Savannah River is named for the Shawnee tribe whose name meant "southerners." Cheraw, Cherokee Falls, Enoree, and Seneca are all named for tribes. Cherokee is a Muskogee word meaning "people of a different speech." Catawba is a Choctaw word for "divided."

SOUTH DAKOTA

Dakota is a Sioux word meaning "allies."

Tribes in the past: Teton Dakota, Yankton Dakota, and the Arikara, who got their name, which means "horn," because they wore their hair sticking up like two horns.

Now: The Dakotas of many different bands live on several large reservations, and there are also some Blackfeet on one reservation.

Names: Sioux is from a Chippewa word meaning "enemy." Sisseton, one of the Dakota tribes, means "swamp village." Huron is the French name of a Great Lakes tribe and means "wild boar."

TENNESSEE

Tennessee is the name of an old Cherokee settlement in the state.

Tribes in the past: Mound Builder, Tennessee, Cherokee, and Chickasaw.

Now: No tribes.

Names: Tullahoma is "rest town." Etowah is the name of an old Cherokee town. The meaning of Etowah has been forgotten, and so has the meaning of another Cherokee word, Chattanooga.

TEXAS

Texas is an Indian word meaning "friendship."

Tribes in the past: Mound Builder, Caddo, Comanche, Kiowa, Tonkawa, Attacapa, Karankawa, Coahuiltec.

Now: A few Alabamas and Coushattas live here.

Names: Cisco means "oily trout." Pecos gets its name from a band the Spanish called "*pecos*" or "shepherd" Indians. Waco gets its name from a Caddo band. Waxahachie is "cow town."

UTAH

Utah is named for the Ute Indians who lived there.

Tribes in the past: Basket Maker, Cliff Dweller, Ute, Paiute, Goshute, Shoshone, and Navaho.

Now: Several hundred Utes and Navahos and a much smaller number of Paiutes, Goshutes, and Shoshones are on reservations.

Names: Uintah is "pine land." Kanab means "willow."

VERMONT

Tribes in the past: Penacook, Mohican and other tribes hunted here, but no tribe lived here as a permanent home.

Now: No tribes.

Names: Winooski is "beautiful river." Missisquoi is "big river." Passumpsic is "much clear water."

VIRGINIA

Tribes in the past: Powhatan, Tuscarora, Tutelo, Monacan, Cherokee.

Now: A few Indians who are descendants of the Powhatans, including some Chickahominies, Mattaponis and Pamunkeys.

Names: The Roanoke River is named for a kind of shell used for money. Onancock is "foggy place." The Shenandoah is "sprucy stream." The Rappahannock is "river of quick rising water." Quantico is "place of dancing." Nottoway means "enemy." You might think the Rapidan River got its name from the Indians. But actually it was named for the English Queen Anne. It is the "rapid Anne." Appomattox is "tobacco plant country."

WASHINGTON

Tribes in the past: Makah, Quinault, Chehalis, Chinook, Kwallioqua, Twana, Nisqualli, Columbia, Yakima, Cœur d'Alêne, Palus.

Now: Remnants of most of these tribes, or of subdivisions of them, live here on reservations. The largest group of tribes belongs to the Salish group of Indians. Some of them are the Snohomish, Clallam, Lummi, Swinomish, and Puyallup.

Names: Chehalis means "inlanders." Chelan is "deep water." The Hoquiam was a river that was said to be "hungry for wood" because a great deal of driftwood collected at the river's mouth. Walla Walla is "rapid stream" in the Nez Percé language. Yakima means "black bear." Tacoma means "mountain." Seattle is named for a chief. Spokane is named for a tribe and means "children of the sun."

WEST VIRGINIA

Tribes in the past: Mound Builder. West Virginia is the only state that was not inhabited by Indians when white men first visited there.

Now: No tribes.

Names: Moundsville is named for the huge earth mound built here by prehistoric Mound Builder Indians. Red Jacket is named for a famous Seneca chief. The Kanawha River is named for a tribe. Buckhannon means "brick river." Many villages are named for tribes.

WISCONSIN

Wisconsin is a Sauk word that refers to the holes in the banks of streams in which birds have their nests.

Tribes in the past: Mound Builder, Winnebago, Kickapoo, Sauk-Fox, Chippewa, and Sioux.

Now: Menominees, Oneidas, Winnebagos, Stockbridges, Munsees and Chippewas have reservations here.

Names: Algoma means "Algonquin waters." Antigo is "evergreen." Kaukauna is "portage." Kewaunee is "wild duck." Manitowoc is "spirit land." Menasha means "island." Mosinee means "moose." Oconomowoc means "beaver." Oconto is "place of pickerel." Ogema means "great grief." Peshtigo is "wild-goose river." Sauk City is named for the tribe. Pewaukee is "lake of shells." Sheboygan may mean "a great noise coming underground from the region of Lake Superior was heard at this place." Wabeno means "eastern men." Wauwatosa means "firefly."

WYOMING

Wyoming is from a Delaware word meaning "large plains."

Tribes in the past: Cheyenne, Arapahoe, Crow, and Shoshone.

Now: Arapahoes and Shoshones live on the Wind River Reservation.

Names: Cheyenne is a Sioux word meaning "foreigners." The Teton (meaning "prairie dwellers") and Gros Ventre (meaning "big belly") Mountains are named for tribes. The Absaroka Mountains get their name from the name the Crow Indians called themselves. And it means "crow." Niobrara means "running water." Uinta County is named for a Ute band and means "pine land."

INDEX